PRESENTATION MANAGEMENT

The New Strategy for Enterprise Content

By

AlexAnndra Ontra
&
James Ontra

Contents

CHAPTER 1 5
The End of PowerPoint Culture 5
What's Wrong with PowerPoint (As If You Didn't Know Already) 6
Introducing: The Discipline of Presentation Management 10
Why Presentation Management is Important Now 13
Millennials in the Workforce 13
Corporate Decentralization 14
The Rise of Artificial Intelligence 15
How Presentation Management Empowers Presenters 16
Productivity 16
Confidence 17
CHAPTER 1 - TAKEAWAYS 18

CHAPTER 2 19
Presentations: From One-and-Done to Enterprise Assets 19
Presentations as Enterprise Assets – The Strategic Approach 21
Presentation Management Increases Productivity 21
Make your team in the field more productive 22
Elevate the value of the content creators 24
Presentation Management Ensures Compliance 25
CHAPTER 2 – TAKEAWAYS 27

CHAPTER 3 28
Enterprise Files for Everyday Use: Components of Presentation Management 28
Components of Presentation Management 28
Central Cloud Location 28
Active Files 29

- Slide Library 30
- Visualization of Files 31
- Search 31
- How Presentation Management Transforms Content 32
- Interactive Presentations 33
- Better Storytelling 35
- The Next Step: Making Presentations Intelligent 36
- Machine Learning and Modeling 37
- CHAPTER 3 - TAKEAWAYS 37

CHAPTER 4 38
- Culture of Presentation Management 38
- Director of Presentation Management 39
- Promote the Benefits – It's PM for *Them* 40
- Show Them It's Familiar: "You Already Know How to Do This" 40
- Training Starts the Conversation 42
- Launch in Phases 44
- Collect Content 45
- CHAPTER 4 – TAKEAWAYS 46

CHAPTER 5 47
- Lifecyle of a Presentation 47
  - Presentation Creation 48
  - Distribution 50
  - Sharing 54
  - Presenting 55
  - Social 56
  - Reporting 57
  - Updating 58
- CHAPTER 5 - TAKEAWAYS 59

- CHAPTER 6 60
  - Making Better Presentations; Telling Better Stories 60
  - Presentations Are the Stories for Business 60
  - Make It Relevant. Ask So What? 61
  - Keep It Short. The 10-Minute Rule. 62
  - Make It Memorable 62
  - How to Create a Story for Business – Formatted to Present ... 64
  - Every presentation is a story. Every slide is a scene 66
  - Content Organization 66
  - CHAPTER 6 - TAKEAWAYS 67
- CHAPTER 7 69
  - The Future of Presentations 69
  - The Humanity of Presentations: Cave Paintings to PowerPoint and Back Again 72
  - Now the Presentation Follows the Conversation 74
- ACKNOWLEDGMENTS 76

CHAPTER 1

The End of PowerPoint Culture

"Yay! I'm going to create a PowerPoint presentation today. I can't wait to get to work," said no one, ever.

But that's about to change. There is an entirely new way to make, manage, use and even *think* about the slides and decks that are so critical to businesses and other organizations.

A new discipline called *presentation management* is bringing decades-old presentation technology into the 21st century. In short, presentation management stores and manages slides in the cloud, so the slides can easily be re-used, shared, updated, tracked and organized for the whole enterprise. The slides become smart – embedded with data and analytics so you can actually gauge their performance. Machine-learning technology can learn about the slides in the system, understand what's happening during a live presentation, and suggest slides to help the presenter instantly find a slide that matches the conversation in the room.

Most importantly, presentation management is a state of mind. It flips the very notion of a presentation on its head, making it more natural – like the way people used to talk and tell stories long before PowerPoint was invented. Slide decks force us to build rigid presentations that we must follow in order, no matter how the room is reacting or what questions get raised. (How many times have you heard: "Hold on, I'll get to that slide in a minute," when someone asks a question?) Presentation management solves this problem. With presentation management, the slides follow the conversation instead of the other way around. Discuss a point, and the right supportive slide appears. Take a turn into an unplanned side topic, and the slides go along for the ride.

Instead of *presenting* in meetings – which is a one-way lecture that quickly gets boring – this new approach means we will actually talk to each other, and always have the right supportive materials at the ready.

A growing number of companies are embracing a presentation management strategy. They range from U.S. Bank to Royal Caribbean Cruise Line to major media companies, consulting groups and medical research labs. Companies that adopt presentation management find they get immediate benefits. They are also putting in place a system for changing the culture of presentations and making them more effective for years to come.

In the presentation management era, the dread of making, giving – or enduring! – a PowerPoint presentation can all but disappear.
This, then, is the story of presentation management and a guide on how to adopt it, make it work, and use it to drive change in your presentation culture.

What's Wrong with PowerPoint (As If You Didn't Know Already)

Like it or not, PowerPoint is the lowest common denominator for business communications. Sure, you can argue that email and instant messaging tools like Slack are used every minute of every day, but critical ideas that require planning and action always make their way into a presentation, usually a PowerPoint deck – or some alternative, like Google Slides. If a business idea has any gravity, it is in a presentation somewhere within the company network.

Yet PowerPoint, which was created over 30 years ago, hasn't changed all that much. It may have gotten fancier, with smarter graphics and cooler animations, and it's pretty easy to use, which is why everyone uses it. But for companies, the fact that everyone is using it is a problem.

Inside most companies, PowerPoint is a tangled nightmare – like old wiring behind the walls just waiting to short-circuit. Too many people use too many decks with too many messages that are out of date, don't match, or even conflict with each other. Need a critical slide at the last second? Good luck finding it. Over 30 million PowerPoint presentations are created every day, constantly adding to the knotty buildup of slides and decks sitting on individual hard drives.

Clearly, there needs to be a better way – a way that takes advantage of innovative technologies like cloud and machine learning – for a company to manage such an important asset.

Presentations are for people who need to understand, act and react. That's how things get done in business. Every business discipline, whether sales, training, research, investor relations, product development or human resources, relies on PowerPoint as a way to reinforce important messages. The CEO's five-year projection, the salesperson's pitch to a prospect, the brand director's marketing plan, the trainer's lecture to a group of new hires working to get certified – they all use PowerPoint to get their message across.

This holds true across industries. Financial institutions rely on decks packed with detailed data to raise money, announce quarterly earnings, present research analysis and market trends, and to communicate portfolio gains and losses to their clientele. Travel and hospitality reps use presentations with glorious photos and videos of their luxurious properties in exotic locations to convince travel agents and potential customers that they should spend their limited free time there. What better way to sell a vacation than to show a sandy beach with crystal blue water? Media companies rely on presentations with authentic pictures of their target consumer, combined with charts describing how their network delivers that very same person. Consultants like McKinsey & Co. and Gartner Inc., generate hundreds of millions of dollars selling their decks of research, analysis and forecasts to their corporate clients. The military is known for its reliance on PowerPoint decks. The most notorious is Gen. Stanley McChrystal's slide that he used at a military briefing in 2009 to describe the complexity of the situation in Afghanistan. "When we understand that slide, we'll have won the war," he said at the time.

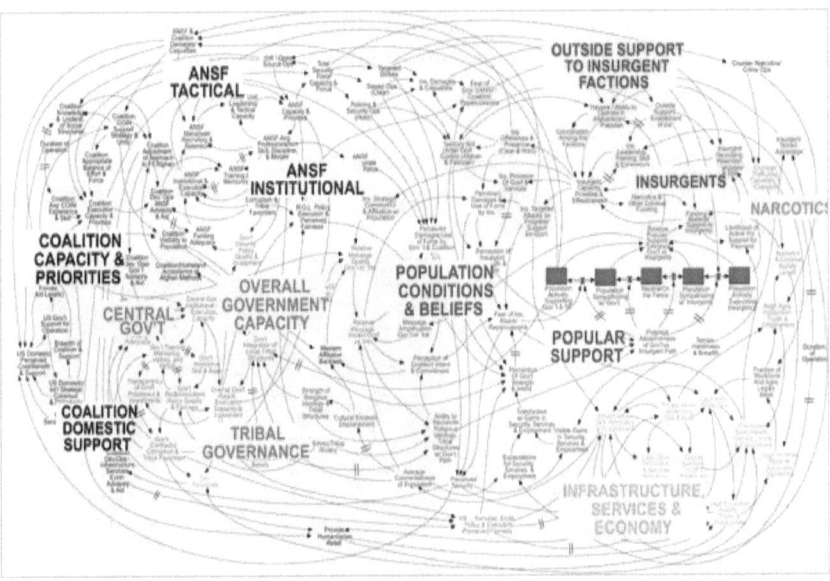

Source: https://www.nytimes.com/2010/04/27/world/27powerpoint.html

McChrystal's slide, though, shows why we rely on PowerPoint so much: It is visual.

Hear a piece of information and, three days later, you will remember 10 percent of it. Add a picture and you'll remember 65 percent. A good 90 percent of the information processed by the brain is visual, according to the book *Brain Rules* by Dr. John Medina. Visual slides are absolutely critical to getting a message across, especially when the stakes are high.

Visual storytelling is powerful and ancient. Throughout the course of history, literacy rates have been abysmally low. It was not until fairly recently, in 2015, that world literacy rates rose to 86.2 percent. In the Stone Age, Neanderthals used cave drawings to communicate with each other. One theory is that the artists described themselves and the animals around them, communicating information that helped them survive. The cave drawings were visual stories relaying critical information.

Visual communications media evolved from cave drawings to paint brushed on wood or stone, to charcoal or ink on paper, then to framed paintings and stained-glass windows. Medieval paintings tell stories of God's glory and wrath, kings decorated with riches and peasants tilling the fields. In a world where most people could not read, the visuals told the stories and taught proper behavior so that everyone could live in a civil society. Visual stories were how human beings evolved and thrived as a dominant species.

Visuals are also a *faster* way to communicate than words alone. Humans are visual first, verbal second. We process visuals 60,000 times faster than text. Let's try an experiment.

Read this: Laughing baby.

No look at this picture:

What induced more of a reaction, the words "laughing baby" or the picture of a laughing baby? Most likely, you had a stronger reaction to the latter -- maybe a bigger smile and a little gasp of, "Aww, how cute!" Pictures evoke emotion where words cannot.

Marketers know this. The advertising industry was built on this. In business, the visuals and graphics that helped sell a product or service were long the purview of skilled tradesmen. Illustrators, typesetters, photographers, retouchers and movie directors were esteemed artisans. They were paid handsomely by corporate marketing-advertising experts to help visualize -- i.e., tell -- the corporate story because businesses saw the importance of conveying the "right" visual story.

Today, media is digital and on-demand. We shoot video instantly on our phones, edit it ourselves, and upload it to YouTube. Pictures can also be taken and retouched right on our phones. Talk about controlling your visual story. We are all the spin-masters of our visual lives.

The ubiquity of digital tools is progress. It's faster and cheaper than ever to take and distribute a beautiful picture. And it's faster and cheaper than ever to create your own deck, rather than spend the time and money hiring someone else to do it. While that's a huge advance, the reliance on PowerPoint has some drawbacks to communications for any kind of organization.

PowerPoint is rigid. It forces the speaker and the audience into a linear train of thought. But as humans, our minds and conversations like to wander. It's how we create and ideate. PowerPoint's linear format forces us into an unnatural thought process. It deters creativity.

Bullet points and the outline format inhibit the narrative. An outline has long been a way to organize thoughts and build a compelling story and conversation around them. It was a starting point to a more in-depth proposal and plan. With PowerPoint, the outline has evolved into the final plan. The nuance and critical thinking that was once the meat of the proposal has now been omitted from "the deck." After all, writing is thinking.

It's a crutch that makes us lazy. If you can get away with a few bullet points, why bother with all that extra thinking work? It's a lot faster to write up some bullets without having to worry about those pesky transitions that tie ideas together. Throw in some nice effects, a few pictures, charts and…*voila*! You're good to go. Yes, you are good to go and bore the hell out your colleagues or clients – the very people on whom your success depends.

There are enough graphics to be dangerous. PowerPoint's greatest attribute is also its worst crime against the critical, thoughtful exchange of ideas. It has a wealth of animated effects, transitions, template designs, charting and graphic tools that will turn a neophyte into a bad graphic designer. Graphs and images, when used to support your main idea, are invaluable. The pitfall lies when users get carried away and use too many images or images that don't necessarily reinforce their idea. So the slides become a distraction from the main point.

It's one and done. A great presentation may take hours or even weeks to create. It might include copywriting, branded graphics, pictures and video that reinforce the message, as well as input from the company's top executives – making it a very powerful piece of communications. This is the kind of content that, when unleashed across the company, can up everyone's game. But after the meeting, this deck gets lost in a folder or some long email chain, to die a lonely death in obscurity. If someone in the company wants to reuse any of that content, then she will spend hours hunting and pecking around the network, opening, scrolling, then closing the wrong files. And if she is lucky enough to stumble upon the right deck, then she will scroll, copy and paste into a new deck. Repeat that seemingly innocuous process several times, and before you know it, there are 20-plus PowerPoint files open on your desktop and you're afraid to close them lest you lose something important. Which file was that? Not sure, so you just save as version 27, which just so happens to be the same as version 25. But no one has the time or energy to read through all those decks that are basically the same. A gross waste of time, money and space -- both mental space and network space.

These presentations become lost assets. Who loses assets? Businesses that fail, that's who! Who uses their assets wisely? Businesses that succeed. Presentations are often overlooked assets, a wellspring of knowledge just waiting to be tapped. Exploiting your presentation assets in a methodical way will improve everyone's performance.

Introducing: The Discipline of Presentation Management

The new discipline of presentation management can have an enormous impact on a company.

Presentation management takes presentations from one-and-done, single files and turns them into enterprise assets deployed intelligently throughout your organization.

Presentation management is a combination of technology and strategic thinking about presentations. We're writing this book because we have been building and rebuilding presentation technologies since the mid-1990s, and we've helped companies understand how to use it to change their thinking about presentations and manage that content as they would any valuable asset. We'll dive deeper into these topics in the following chapters, but briefly, presentation management works like this:
A company decides that it wants to use its presentation content over and over again, rather than waste time and money re-creating slides that already exist but no one can seem to find. So the company engages a presentation management service to store and track these files and slides.

When employees need to create a new presentation, they log into the service, do a quick search for the specific content they need, and preview their options from a variety of formats, including PowerPoint, video, images and PDFs. Then they just select the slides needed for the new deck. It's like shopping online: You log in, browse for stuff, and click on what you want. Except instead of putting stuff into a shopping cart, they are moving slides or other files into a slide tray that gets saved as a new presentation, which they can then use in their next meeting.

On the back end, the company has a record of who used which slides and videos, just as Amazon knows that you bought shampoo and a book last week. That's presentation management in its simplest form. But most large enterprises take the discipline further and develop a more strategic approach to presentations.

U.S. Bank is one example. The fifth-largest bank in the U.S. had challenges with its presentations that should sound familiar to any big corporation. Each department was its own presentation silo. There was no consistent branding across the decks made by people in different units, and the corporate marketing team had little control over who presented what to whom. Employees making their own decks were presenting products that didn't exist anymore, or using variations of the brand that had long since been retired. On top of that, it was taking their employees a good five hours each to create their presentations. They were looking through a SharePoint site and network folders, opening and scrolling through random decks to copy and paste slides into a new, patchwork deck. Some decks had different backgrounds; others just had bad or old information. So countless employees wasted piles of time creating inaccurate, noncompliant (which in banking means risking the rage of regulators) slides.

Their presentation process, or lack thereof, was too rogue for a 150-year-old institution with about half a trillion dollars in assets. So U.S. Bank implemented a presentation management strategy to provide better branded content to its teams -- and take outdated content out of circulation so no one could present the wrong information ever again.

To do that, the bank contracted with us at Shufflrr to provide a cloud presentation solution. Just giving employees the ability to find the right slides and drag and drop them into presentations cut down the time required to create presentations from five hours to five minutes, U.S. Bank executive Scott Welvaert tells us. Shufflrr also comes with a variety of controls, such as permissions, updates and metrics. Corporate marketing can give access to those people who are qualified to use and present certain content. Each division can control its content for its team. If someone needs to cross-sell a product from another division, that person can easily be given access. Corporate administrators can push out updated content, which ensures that old material gets retired and every slide is up to date.

Finally, thanks to reporting and metrics, corporate marketing can see what content gets used most often and by whom. U.S. Bank finally got real data about its content and how or whether it resonates with customers or others who are on the receiving end of presentations.

It's important to note that U.S. Bank's presentation management solution was not just a tool with some cool features that let it arrange and control content. Adopting the technology also forced the bank's leadership team to think about presentations in a different way. Marketing could create a corporate encyclopedia of U.S. Bank content sourced from the experts in each division, for use by the entire U.S. Bank team. It was a top-down approach that still gives individuals autonomy and flexibility to do their particular job, and do it well.

The result: U.S. Bank corporate finally had control over the brand and product message, while employees had a faster, easier way to create presentations. Presentation management is a win-win for all sides of the enterprise.

That is the competitive advantage of presentation management. It unleashes all of the great knowledge within your company's presentations. By employing an intelligent presentation management strategy, you are giving everyone in your company the ability to talk intelligently about any aspect of the business at any time, whether or not it is their particular area of expertise. Everyone becomes as knowledgeable and articulate as the CEO. (And we'll talk more about that later.) But that's only part of the equation. By employing a presentation management strategy, you are also mitigating risk and increasing productivity.

Why Presentation Management is Important Now

Three different waves of change are merging to profoundly affect how corporations operate. The first is the flood of Millennials into the workforce, and how that generation consumes media and technology. The second is decentralization of corporate hierarchy. The third is the arrival of artificial intelligence, or AI. Though seemingly disparate, these three elements are converging like different cold and warm fronts to combine into the perfect storm. Presentation management will help your company navigate that storm.

Millennials in the Workforce

Millennials – the generation born from 1981 to 1997 -- will make up 75 percent of the workforce by 2025, and they are bringing their media and tech habits into the workplace. Millennials grew up digital. They are the first generation raised with mobile phones and social media. They live through their devices. Not only do they socialize with friends through apps and Instagram, but they watch TV on iPads, order food online, and send texts and email on their phones. Not surprisingly, they are also multitaskers with several browser windows open on their laptops along with a messaging app, and a smartphone chiming away with constant alerts. Their eyes and thoughts are accustomed to moving from one screen and idea to the next and then back again. They spend three or more hours a day looking at their phones, accustomed to instant gratification. And those same habits carry over to their professional lives.

Presentation management meshes slides and decks with this Millennial mentality. A typical PowerPoint deck is linear -- slide one, slide two, slide three. It is a preplanned deck – and, so, a preplanned talk -- with little room for spontaneous discussion. Millennials like to get information in an interactive, multi-threaded way. Presentation management makes presenting more interactive. From a Millennial standpoint, they're thinking, "I have a question about your product, and I'd like it answered now, without having to sit through 30 more slides until you get to it." Presentation management encourages a fluid exchange of ideas – with supporting visuals -- during a meeting. It lets the presentation follow the conversation – a massively important point that we'll dive into later.

Corporate Decentralization

Corporate structure and culture has been profoundly changing for years. Corporations are shifting from a hierarchical structure, to a decentralized, more autonomous workforce. Jamie Dimon, CEO of the largest American bank, JPMorgan Chase & Co., stated in a public letter, "Bureaucracy is a disease. Bureaucracy drives out good people, slows down decision making, kills innovation and is often the petri dish of bad politics." The corner office has gone the way of flannel suits and wingtips. Iconic American companies are moving from suburban areas to city centers. In 2017, General Electric sold its sprawling Fairfield, Conn., campus and moved its headquarters to Boston. In 2018 McDonald's moved from Oak Brook, Ill., into downtown Chicago. Companies are moving into dynamic urban areas because that's where college graduates want to live.

At the same time, working remotely has moved from a perk to an expectation. It is estimated that there has been a 115 percent increase in telecommuting over the last 10 years, and 43 percent of the U.S. workforce works remotely, according to the 2017 study State of Telecommuting in the U.S. Employee Workforce by Global Workplace Analytics. Being tethered to a cubicle is not necessarily the most productive way to get the job done. Workers complain of distractions in the office from things as simple as watercooler chitchat to colleagues walking by and asking for things. Long commutes waste time and pile on stress – the time and energy could be better spent focused on a task. In addition, workers want more flexibility in their schedules so they can balance career and family life. Ubiquitous wireless connectivity makes remote work productive.

Presentation management transcends geography. Whether your company still requires everyone to report into the office or encourages a mobile workforce with lots of flex time, presentation management gives workers high-level content to promote their company and their company's products from anywhere, at any time. Employees can give a presentation over coffee at Starbucks using a phone, or at a podium in a boardroom equipped with giant screens. It gives presenters the flexibility to adjust their message to whatever the client or prospect demands at any given moment, while ensuring the corporate brand and message stay true.

The Rise of Artificial Intelligence

AI is creating new opportunities for business -- and for presentations. Today, companies use AI to analyze data, identify market trends and predict the consumer's next step. A Google search is AI in a primitive form.

AI is starting to make emotional connections for consumers. Let's compare apples and oranges. Categorically, they are both fruit, round, grow on trees, and are available for sale in the produce section. But they are not the same. They look and taste different. Alex uses oranges for fresh juice every morning to get her full day supply of vitamin C, whereas she uses apples for baking pies. Come to think of it, our grandmother made the best apple pie in the entire world. Our grandmother was the most wonderful woman in our entire world, and she always made us feel safe and loved when she tucked us in at night. There is a real difference in how Alex interprets, experiences and interacts with these two kinds of fruit. She associates apples with our grandmother and feelings of love and security, but she sees oranges as just a source of nutrition. AI is increasingly able to make these connections for us – to connect the apple to our grandma to a feeling of being safe and loved. As AI advances, it will recognize these associations and make suggestions accordingly.

From a business presentation standpoint, the same process applies, but with slides. AI in presentation management can recognize patterns in your presentations. Those patterns could be related to the slides you view, present, rank, search for, and any other activity related to slide usage. We call it Predictive Slides™, and it should be a key piece of any presentation management strategy.

The concept works like this:

Let's say you are preparing for a meeting with a client, and you choose 15 slides from your library of 500. The AI behind Predictive Slides can already have some idea of who you are meeting with and what will be discussed.

During that meeting, you find out your client is interested in a different product than anticipated, and the client wants more detailed information. All are positive "buy" signs. So you want to seize this opportunity and present the information the client needs.

Predictive slides can take cues from your actions and slide choices – much the way Google takes cues from your searches – and can surface the right slides at the right time. Instead of having to search for slides about that other product, predictive slides will make the connection, saving the presenter time hunting and scrolling through a 500-slide library.

When this happens in real time, the meeting becomes more productive. You give clients the information they want. It makes you and your company look smarter, which makes the client more likely to buy.

How Presentation Management Empowers Presenters

When we talk about presenters in this book, we are referring to people who want to drive action. In business, this is often the salesperson, but it really can be any leader in the company. Leaders at all levels, from middle management to the C-suite, need to motivate people to act. And whether that "act" means getting someone to buy the company's products, invest capital in the company, contribute great ideas to a project, or learn something new and therefore become a better, more productive employee, presentation management strategy will raise everyone's ability to present better, to act better. Presentation management is empowering because it increases productivity and confidence.

Productivity

As U.S. Bank's Scott Welvaert said, the time required to put together presentations after implementing a presentation management solution dropped from five hours to five minutes. In its most basic form, presentation management empowers presenters to easily find and reuse compliant content for their specific meeting. So the tedious hours employees would have spent searching around the network for existing content or writing and designing content even when that's not their skill set, become a simple keyword search. Type in a few words, find the right slide and drag and drop it into a new presentation. The four hours and 55 minutes saved can be better spent learning more about a particular client and building new relationships with new clients. The presenters have more time to actually conduct their business.

Presentation management gives the marketing and compliance departments – who typically create content -- an effective means to distribute their work, ensure its use and reuse, and track slides and files to see what's resonating in the field. The company can control content to ensure that everyone is using the right, up-to-date content with the proper brand standards, messaging and disclosure statements. Those departments no longer lose days derailed by last-minute requests, "Hey, can you help me find that slide? I have a meeting in 20 minutes and I need some data on product AA."

Confidence

A smart presentation management strategy ensures a content repository that is accessible on the fly. Wherever you are, whomever you are with, it gives you quick access to critical company information. You are empowered to speak intelligently, and correctly, about any aspect of your company's business. All good salespeople prepare for meetings, of course. They study their client's business and study the company's products to ensure that they are offering – presenting -- the best solution for that client. But clients throw curve balls. There's always that one question, "Our problem isn't so much about AA but really about BB." Even if you've spent weeks researching AA for this meeting, with presentation management, you can switch gears and discuss BB with that client. All the BB content is accessible. So as a speaker, you don't have to miss a beat.

With that arsenal of company information supporting you, you don't have to bluff or give that meeting-killer response, "I'll get back to you on that later." You can instead lead a deep, interactive discussion with your client. When the client asks a question, whether you were prepared for it or not, you can still answer correctly and intelligently. Question and answer leads to more discussion, more active participation from the client. When the client is talking, you are learning more about her business. What you home in on from her feedback, you can then turn into a better solution, and tell a better story about how you can help them – a story that sells.

So now you've spent less time creating a riveting and compliant presentation that actually encourages deeper discussion with your client. Through this process, you've built more credibility and trust. Clients who trust you buy from you. Colleagues who trust you work harder for and with you.

Who in your company communicates instinctively, naturally? The CEO. CEOs can field any question about any aspect of the business, right off the cuff. They are charismatic, natural storytellers who motivate those around them, whether they are customers, investors or employees. Their knowledge affords them credibility. Their stories inspire. That's why they get named as CEOs!

A well-executed presentation management strategy helps everyone at the company speak with the dexterity of the CEO. It combines the detailed information needed to inform, with the storytelling needed to inspire and the flexibility to present anywhere, anytime, with anyone – just like a skilled CEO.

CHAPTER 1 - TAKEAWAYS

1. Presentations are made to communicate important ideas and motivate people to act. The actions could be to make a purchase, learn something new, or participate in a project. They are created to move someone to do something.
2. Most companies have a mess of PowerPoint and other files tangled on their networks. Embedded in these files is great information, but no one can find it. Presentations are a grossly wasted resource.
3. Presentation management takes one-and-done files and transforms them into enterprise assets.
4. Presentation management empowers presenters by giving them more confidence and making them more productive.
5. Visual communications are more powerful than words alone. We respond to pictures, especially pictures that depict emotion.

CHAPTER 2

Presentations: From One-and-Done to Enterprise Assets

In a meeting room at ABC National Television Sales in 2006 – before the iPhone, before cheap thumb drives, before easy cloud storage – we learned a hard lesson about PowerPoint presentations and the pace of technological change. That lesson started us on our journey to develop the concept of enterprise presentation management.

We are a brother-sister team, and we have been consulting with enterprise clients, providing presentation technology and creative services for over 20 years.

James worked at a boutique agency called Micro Interactive. One of the agency's early customers was CBS Networks, which bought an advertising sales presentation solution to help sell its sponsorships for the 1998 Nagano Olympics. Broadcasters were early adopters of presentation technology – because there is no better way to sell TV sponsorships than with images and video.

In the 1990s, video running on a laptop was pretty cutting edge. From broadcasters, the trend toward presentations that incorporated graphics, animation, video and sound spread to other enterprises.

Micro Interactive built a pretty nice business designing and developing custom sales solutions – and Micro Interactive was soon purchased by the web development company iXL in the midst of the late-1990s dot-com boom. James joined iXL as head of sales for multimedia services, and later spun out his division into a new company, Iguana Interactive. AlexAnndra left her advertising agency career to join Iguana Interactive. (This is how we wound up working together. Our mother is so happy.) In the first 18 months, Iguana Interactive developed and designed presentation solutions for clients such as the National Basketball Association, the National Football League, Comedy Central, American Express, Kelly Services, Bravo, De Beers and Mercedes-Benz. Not a bad roster for a start-up. Unfortunately, when the dot-com bubble burst in 2001, so did Iguana Interactive's. The investors decided to close shop and walk away.

After 9/11, in a depressed New York City, we metaphorically (and maybe even physically) pulled Iguana out of the dumpster. James was the final creditor to Iguana Interactive, so he traded his employment contract for the Iguana software. With two borrowed desks, a phone and a ping pong table that doubled as a conference table, we started Ontra Presentations. We cold-called old clients, who were pissed that Iguana closed shop on them, and tried to find some new clients. We finally landed ABC National Television Sales.

Yet by then, something interesting was happening to business presentations. The software to make presentations moved from clunky and expensive CDs running locally on laptops and desktops, to software-as-a-service tapped through networks and the cloud. Video that was once expensive to produce and required highly skilled directors and editors turned into a commodity -- anyone could make a video on a smartphone. The entire spectrum of presentation creation got democratized.

And this is what led to the moment at ABC. An exasperated sales rep walked into our meeting and threw a CD on the table. "My grandmother made a nicer presentation for our family reunion than our sales presentation!" OUCH. It became obvious to us that the problem to solve concerning presentations would no longer be how to create them. It would be how to manage all the presentations that would be created by all the individuals at every level of an organization.

We knew we had to build a new solution to keep up with ever more accessible technology and clients' expectations.

And yet, we also realized that while technology had changed, the reason our clients called us in the first place remained the same. For almost 30 years, clients across all industries have listed their presentation problems as:

1. There is no compliance or consistency of message across the team.
2. No one knows what all of the employees are presenting and to whom.
3. It takes too long to prepare presentations for meetings.

In short, enterprises want more control over the presentation content while making managers, salespeople, marketers and anyone else who relies on presentations more productive.

And so, we developed the discipline of presentation management and built technology to support it – and have continued to learn from clients who adopt presentation management so we can constantly improve and update our approach. Clearly, the era of one-and-done decks is over.

Instead, smart organizations apply presentation management to create and manage decks like enterprise assets.

Presentations as Enterprise Assets – The Strategic Approach

It is time to usher in long-term thinking about presentation objectives. A company's best presentations combine the best ideas from top leadership with professional writing, sleek graphics and precise branding. Presentations are a form of branding. That can benefit everyone in the company over the long term, rather than just a few people in one meeting.

Presentation management positively affects everyone in the company, from the C-suite to the field manager. In fact, companies that adopt robust enterprise content management and presentation management strategies stand to realize a 400 percent ROI within five years of adoption, according to research by information management company M-Files. In order to transition from a "one-and-done" presentation mentality to an enterprise strategy, organizations must think differently about their strategic communications and presentations.

Simply put, ***presentations are strategic communications***, and they deserve the same discipline and strategic approach as other elements in the communications mix. Think about how your company approaches PR, social, digital, advertising – with set objectives, planning, production, execution and measurement. Presentations should be no different.

Presentation Management Increases Productivity

Make your content productive
The core benefit of presentation management is the ability to create great content once, and then make it available to anyone in the organization to use over and over again. Typically, that content is a PowerPoint deck, but it could also be a video, PDF brochure, white paper or infographic. The format doesn't matter. What matters is the ability to take any piece of content and unleash it across the organization.

Consider the cost of paying all those highly skilled marketers, writers, designers, producers, analysts and other subject matter experts to plan, produce, execute, measure and then revise presentation content. It adds up to an estimated $1 billion per year. Organizations are making a monumental investment in their content. Unfortunately, some 70 percent of content created by marketing goes unused, according to Translations GlobalLink. And over 90 percent is never reused. Companies are squandering $900 million of marketing assets annually. Yikes!

Put that content to work. Put it in a cloud location, where presenters can easily find what they need and drop it into decks. That will get you a better return on your marketing investment. An effective presentation management strategy will direct the best content to the employees who need it, when they need it. Presentation management will make it easy for the user to find files and slides, and then repurpose them for their meeting. They don't have to start from scratch re-creating a slide that already exists somewhere, if only they could find it. It also means presenters can access content when they are actually in the meeting, face to face with the client. So when the client throws a curve-ball question that the presenter hadn't anticipated, she can go to the presentation library on the fly and present content that answers the client's question. She doesn't have to "wing it" or tell the client that she'll send that info over later.

Presentation management means the right content is directed to the right person at the right time. So naturally, the content gets used more – and more effectively. The more content gets used, the more value it has. Presentation management gives a higher return on your company's investment in content.

Make your team in the field more productive

If the content is more productive, the team will be more productive as well.

Client feedback has told us that presentation management can save two to five hours in preparation for a meeting. Royal Caribbean Cruises Lines estimated that their presentation management solution saved 300 business managers 2.5 hours per presentation. Multiply that over 50 weeks, and you've just unleashed an additional 86,000 hours of productive time. That's time that can be spent building relationships with clients and partners, solving clients' unique problems, innovating for the company, or working on initiatives that actually build the business, as opposed to the tedious administrative task of creating a new deck that already exists somewhere.

Every sales person saved 5 hours per week

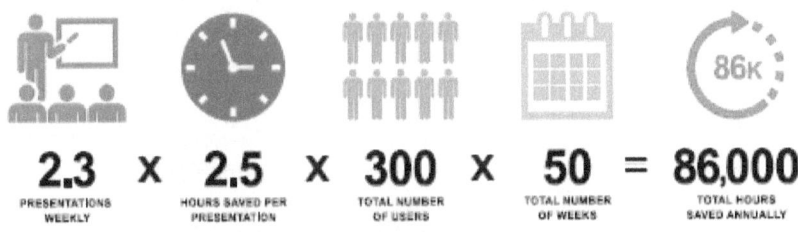

2.3 × 2.5 × 300 × 50 = 86,000
PRESENTATIONS WEEKLY / HOURS SAVED PER PRESENTATION / TOTAL NUMBER OF USERS / TOTAL NUMBER OF WEEKS / TOTAL HOURS SAVED ANNUALLY

* Source: Royal Caribbean International Case Study

Presentation management takes workers out of their cubicles and puts them back into the world. But what happens when they are already face to face with a client, partner or other colleague? It lets them approach presentations in an entirely new way.

The presentation follows the conversation. The best salespeople listen, then respond and react to what their clients are conveying. A one-and-done slideshow forces the speaker into a rigid, linear story with little room for spontaneity or creativity. But successful business is conducted through relationships, and relationships are built through interactive dialogue – a volley where both sides share and build on each other's last comment.

Today, when a real discussion starts in a meeting, the slideshow is typically left behind. One slide just languishes, ignored on the monitor. Presentation management allows on-demand access to a comprehensive library where users can actually search and present a slide or file. When the client redirects the conversation, i.e., the presentation, the presenter can present the content accordingly. And this content is already compliant and up-to-date.

So the presenter can follow through with the right materials and advance the relationship. No longer does he need to schedule another follow-up meeting, or chase the client down for the next couple of months to get that second (or third, fourth or even fifth) meeting. The presenter can address all of the issues on the spot.

Presentation management reduces the number of meetings and time needed to close a deal, allowing the rep to chase more deals in the same time frame. Furthermore, when you can answer a client's question on the spot, you look smarter, and are smarter. You build credibility for yourself and for the company. Trust builds long-term profitable relationships.

Elevate the value of the content creators

When the content generates a higher return on investment, and your team is more productive because of how they are using that content, then that trickles right up the ladder to the content creators themselves. From the writers to the designers to the strategists and producers, many people from different disciplines contribute to a piece of marketing collateral. Presentation management increases the value of their work and how it's perceived across the organization.

As a high-level example, let's consider materials prepared for a huge conference, where the CEO is the keynote speaker. The budget and profile is typically pretty big for such an event, easily running into the six figures. The marketing department creates a presentation, using professional copywriters, graphic designers and animators. Other department leaders also contribute content. Then, perhaps, a video is produced – again with professional writers, directors, videographers, makeup artists, etc. The costs keep rising.

With presentation management, elements of that presentation can be reused and repurposed, quickly and easily.

We're not implying that everyone in the company can give the CEO's keynote presentation. But with a presentation management strategy in place, it will be much easier and more common for the rest of the company to reuse and repurpose assets from that presentation for their own meetings.

The same results hold true on a more mundane level, since we know that most presentations don't have a $100,000 budget and are not given by the CEO. A presentation created for a sales call is actually used multiple times across the entire sales team. The content creators' product affects 300 people in the company over the course of a year, versus two people in the company over the course of one meeting. With presentation management, the effort of content creators is elevated from a one-and-done tactical exercise to a strategic initiative benefiting the entire organization. In so doing, the content creators get more exposure and contribute more value throughout the company.

On top of that, presentation management directs the content to the presenters in the field. The content creators field fewer last-minute, panicked requests, like:

> "Hey, I have a meeting in one hour, where is the new pricing?"
> "I can't find the slide!"
> "Do you mind, just, putting these few slides together for me?"

Marketing puts out these fires every day. Every time a last-minute request comes in, everything else drops. The day is derailed. Worse, the day is derailed by a request for something that already exists! Fewer fires to put out means the marketing team can put their resources to strategic initiatives that build the brand and push the business forward.

Presentation Management Ensures Compliance

Compliance can mean different things to different organizations. In finance and pharma, it means that specific language and statements are disclosed in accordance with federal regulations. You must tell your customers "this" but you are not allowed to tell them "that." What employees can and cannot say is regulated. And "who" can and cannot present certain material is also regulated. In finance, you must be a certified broker-dealer to sell investments. In pharma, you might need to be a medical doctor to educate other doctors about how to administer a particular drug. In marketing, compliance means that you are staying true to the brand, which refers to the colors used, the logo treatment, the fonts and typography, even certain messages and taglines.

Compliance can also mean the products and pricing are up to date. Every industry, every business, every division within that business has rules that they follow, with which they must comply. When we refer to presentation compliance, we are making sure that all of the content presented follows those rules, whatever they may be for your company.

In the discipline of presentation management, compliance is controlled through a number of elements working in concert.

Permissioned access: Who gets access to which content is important for two reasons. First, it ensures that qualified people have access to their information. You wouldn't want a research assistant presenting company financials. That's a lousy way to prove the company is a sound investment opportunity. Second, you don't want the research assistant wasting his time wading through financial content, when what he really needs to do his job are the results of some focus group. Permissions not only protect the company from risk, they direct the employees to the information they need to do their job well.

Forced content: Forced content benefits both legal and marketing. In highly regulated industries like finance and pharmaceuticals, companies are required to include legal disclosure statements with the information they present. If they don't, they will have a regulatory watchdog knocking on their doors and run the risk of expensive and even debilitating lawsuits and fines. From a marketing perspective, you want to be sure that your people are telling the "complete" story about the product and/or the company. So, you *force* certain slides, content, etc. into their presentations.

Organization-wide updates: It's so easy for users to pick up that last version of the deck they used for their last meeting because it's saved on their desktop. They know exactly where it is. It's faster and easier for them. But in doing so, they risk presenting outdated, wrong and noncompliant content. The risk of misinformation could result in a regulatory fine, an angry client and lost revenue. When slides and files are updated by a content administrator or expert, those updates are pushed out to all users, ensuring that everyone stays current -- and therefore compliant.

Reporting: Knowing who is presenting what to whom, when, and in what context provides documented evidence that the company is following regulatory guidelines, maintaining industry compliance, and presenting the complete story. Are your sales reps presenting the latest pricing? Did they include the right disclosure statements? You'll know through reporting.

The road to hell is paved with good intentions. Compliance protocols and processes are fantastic from a high-level enterprise point of view. Yay, control! But the folks on the front lines, working directly with partners and customers need to be flexible, creative, responsive and above all, they cannot wait until "compliance" approves their deck. Boo, bureaucracy! Presentation management balances compliance with productivity. At the end of the day, your workers -- sales reps in particular -- are judged by the quality and quantity of their work, of what they do. Sales reps are measured by how much they sell, not whether they used the right shade of blue in their PowerPoint template or remembered to include the right legalese. Presentation management understands that dynamic so your enterprise can promote its brand while your team can get their job done.

CHAPTER 2 – TAKEAWAYS

1. Presentation management is a strategic approach to presentations, treating them as enterprise assets that can be used over and over again throughout the organization.
2. Presentations are strategic communications that deserve the same level of attention and discipline as branding elements.
3. Presentation management provides a greater ROI on your content because reuse of the content multiplies.
4. Presentation management empowers your team to create better presentations in less time. It makes them more productive.
5. Interactive features let the presentation follow the conversation, unlocking presenters and their audience from rigid, linear slide decks.
6. Presentation compliance refers to legal messaging, marketing messaging and branding elements. It makes sure that everyone's presentations are following the "rules" for that business.

CHAPTER 3

Enterprise Files for Everyday Use: Components of Presentation Management

Presentation management balances both sides of the enterprise: the high-level corporate brand and objectives with the everyday tasks of the employees out in the field -- the folks whose day-to-day tasks are what actually build the business. Presentation management makes enterprise files available for everyday use and vice versa. It's like a merger of content. To achieve this requires three key components: cloud-based technology that can store, update and track presentations; analytics and machine learning that can recognize patterns in and the effectiveness of presentations; and a cultural shift toward thinking about presentations differently.

These components, when combined, will change the nature of presentations in your organization.

Components of Presentation Management

Modern technology is the backbone of a great presentation management strategy. Of course, we at Shufflrr built just such technology and would like to sell it to you. But whether you buy it from someone else or build it yourself, the discipline of presentation management requires a few key elements.

Central Cloud Location

Amazingly, in this era of ubiquitous cloud computing, most companies don't have a central cloud repository of presentation slides. Slides get stored everywhere. Individuals keep decks on their laptops. Some groups might share a Google Drive or dump presentations into a shared Dropbox account. Some companies used SharePoint's Slide Library, which has been discontinued. But whether we're talking about a small business or a *Fortune* 500 corporation, it's rare to find a single, organized, sophisticated cloud solution for presentations.

It might seem obvious, but if slides are scattered in all sorts of pockets of storage, they can't be shared, reused, and monitored for compliance and consistency. The only way to get this party started is to get *all* presentations into one place in one location, preferably a cloud drive that anyone with permission can access.

So, step one: Establish or buy (from us!) a central presentation repository and upload all of the company's presentation files. Remember, these files are not limited to PowerPoint, they could include video, images, brochure PDFs, etc. When we refer to *presentation files* in this book, we are talking about anything that can be presented.

Step two: Make this library accessible to everyone in your organization with the proper permissions. Permissions are important because they direct users to the content that they need, and they help manage risk and ensure compliance.

Step three: Dedicate a person or group to guide presentation strategy and direction. The presentation directors are responsible for ensuring that the presentation management strategy is planned and implemented in your company. Think of it like an advertising director who is responsible for all of the development, execution and measurement of the company's advertising, or an event manager who is responsible for selecting the conferences and ensuring that the right employees are attending with the right collateral. We'll go deeper into what skill set a director of presentation management should have in the next chapter. But for now, our point is that someone in the company should own the presentation strategy.

Active Files

Once presentations are in the cloud, the next step is to make them "active." That means making them visual, searchable, accessible and reusable. They are permissioned, and their use is tracked. Visual files are files that are formatted to present. You can preview for yourself and present them to a client all from the same place. Search is a pretty standard feature but we all know that some search engines are better than others at helping you find content you need. Combine search with visualized results and you've instantly solved one problem: how to help employees find the right slides for their decks.

Accessible files are ones that your team can get to easily. Permissions enable accessibility because they direct users to content that is relevant to their job. And finally, reusable files refer to the ability to take a file or slide from a file and put it in a new presentation without a lot of hassle. For our clients, we provide a tray where users can drag and drop files and slides, put them in order, and then save them out as a new file. It's like an Amazon shopping cart, except you are shopping for slides, and other content, instead of stuff.

In contrast, the opposite of active files are dormant files -- files that are hidden, asleep on your network somewhere and are hard to find. Active files, on the contrary, are ready to work -- *ready to present* -- from anywhere, anytime. A sales rep presenting at her customer's office can find and access the files and present them within seconds. Or she could share a large-file video with her colleague across town.

Slide Library

Going back to the mid-1990s, every solution we developed for our clients has had a slide library. It's the foundation of presentation strategy. Whether your build one or buy one, a slide library becomes the catalyst for changing files from one-and-done to enterprise assets.

A slide library is a critical component of presentation management because it makes files really easy to reuse. It makes them active. Your employees don't want to just grab a whole presentation and use it as is – rarely does an entire presentation used in one setting fit another time and place. Employees instead need a library of finely crafted, approved slides that they can draw from to create their own presentations for their own situations. In a slide library, your files are broken down into their elements. A PowerPoint deck will show all of the slides separately within that file. So you can pick and choose the slides you want. A video will appear already formatted as a slide, ready to play. The system will show a Word doc or PDF in its entirety, but with each page broken down, so again you can pick and choose which pages you need.

Now, you're probably thinking, I can already do that in PowerPoint and Word -- just highlight what I want and copy and paste into my new file. So what do I need a slide library for?

First, with a slide library all files are formatted and ready to present. You can review all the slides, files, pages, videos, etc. with one click. It lets you preview all files side by side, or toggle easily from one to the other, and then another, without a big mess of 20 open documents cluttering up your desktop screen. So you can find exactly what you are looking for.

Second, once you've found what you're looking for, a slide library has functionality to let you select content efficiently, with drag-and-drop or one-click to select individual slides, videos, etc. into your new presentation. This is much more efficient than scrolling through a bunch of open files on your desktop. You can see it, move it, drag-and-drop it, put it in a specific order, and save it.

Presentation management breaks the larger files down into pieces, so users can access the pieces that they need to customize their new presentation.

Visualization of Files

A key to presentation management is how it *visualizes the files* to make them so much easier to preview and read through.

You can see into slide 35 of an 80-slide deck, or page 76 of a 200-page white paper, right there in the cloud drive, without opening any files or software. The same is true for video and other file types. In Shufflrr, we offer at least five different views in three sizes. Users can view one slide enlarged to full screen, or all of the slides in one presentation, or several presentations next to each other, so they can compare and contrast content. Furthermore, the visualization extends to the new file you are creating. As you mix slides, videos and images, you can see how your new presentation flows and you can make changes accordingly. That seemingly innocuous task can actually save hours in a user's preparation time. Visualization makes the files accessible and active.

With visualization, you can see the file and decide in seconds if it's right for your purpose. It's formatted and ready to present. In presentation management every file is visual, every file is a slide.

Search

In presentation management, search encompasses not just file names and meta tags, but text within the file, titles, body copy, speaker notes, etc., with mechanisms to sort and filter. It's all searchable, and search criteria is customizable. In Shufflrr, all PowerPoint decks are indexed when they are uploaded into the app. Content administrators don't have to do anything extra to make the files searchable.

Let's say you need to create a presentation about cats. Just like when using Google, you input the term "cats" in the search window. Search results return all files, slides and folders with the word "cats" in them. But unlike Google, the results are visual. You get a little preview of each slide or file so you can review it without leaving the page or window, and then you won't have navigate back again if you choose the wrong slide. It's all contained within the same window.

How Presentation Management Transforms Content

Once cloud storage, active files, slide libraries, visualization and search are up and running, anyone at your company can use it to build better presentations using the best content from your best people. And as that discipline spreads throughout your organization, you will notice some very interesting effects on the culture of presentations.

The old idea of one-and-done presentations fades away, and a new culture of reuse takes over. And the more a file and slide are reused, the more productive they become, and the higher the return on your content investment. Here are other ways the concept of presentations changes after the implementation of presentation management.

Employees create new presentations from existing content. They will use a slide or file many times over again in different presentations for different meetings. More bang for your buck. Find the slide and file you need, when you need it, and then create a custom presentation using that file or slide. Presentation management strategy expedites this process.

Internal and external usage gets easier. When companies think enterprise, they think internal for their employees only. That's great for company employees who are collaborating on a project and can all access the material and review it together through the same drive. But presentation management also includes external usage. Those same files, accessible from the same repository, can be shared on-demand with a client or partner outside of the enterprise. Presentation management includes the ability to share and collaborate externally, via shared links, webinars or chats.

Internal and external usage is controlled through permissions and security. So your company can still manage how, where and with whom files and slides are shared. Confidential information will stay that way. One version of the content – one source of truth -- can be used in multiple scenarios. This limits the need for multiple versions in different locations. One enterprise asset, repurposed for different needs.

Presentation management can change the overall meeting experience. Old-school linear presentations, prepared the day before and followed slide by slide, force the presenter to talk *at* his audience. No one likes to be talked at. With accessible files, the presenter can comfortably go "off-slides" because he has the content to support his message. At the same time, the other meeting attendees are encouraged to participate and contribute to the meeting. The result is less proselytizing and more conversation, which means that more information gets shared and everyone is more productive. The presentation follows the conversation.

Interactive Presentations

The cost of creating a successful new drug is anywhere from $650 million to $2 billion. The price tag is so high because the hit rate is so low: 90 percent of drugs developed don't make it to market. Few drugs make it through all three phases of clinical trials, and when they do, they still need to get FDA approval. Most drugs are developed after a huge financial investment, years of clinical testing and trials, and a ton of time invested by a team of passionate medical professionals, scientists and even patients with a genuine interest in curing a disease. And after that arduous process, the approval decision hinges on one presentation to an FDA Advisory Committee.

An Advisory Committee, or AdComm, is a panel of experts with special knowledge of the disease the drug is targeted to treat. The AdComm is usually made up of doctors, scientists, patients and industry and consumer representatives. The stakes are high, so naturally, the panel needs the right information about the drug and its trial results to make good decisions. It's up to the presenter -- the drugmaker -- to give the panel that information during the AdComm review.

We worked with a consultancy called Innovative Science Solutions (ISS) that helps drug and medical device companies get AdComm recommendations for FDA approval. ISS relies on interactive presentations during meetings to do so. All the trial results are compiled into a slide library of more than 1,000 slides. The content tells the entire story of the drug, from its creation in the lab, to its compound structure, its chemical reaction in the human body, as well as the methodology, preparation, execution and results of each clinical trial. The slides include testimonials from patients who participated in the trials. The slide library is like a comprehensive encyclopedic reference for that one drug.

ISS prepares the presentation. It chooses 100 to 200 slides from the library that the Chief Development Officer (CDO) for the drug company will then present to the Advisory Committee.

The AdComm format in and of itself is intense. It is several days with everyone in a hotel conference room or some other neutral location. The CDO presents a formal, linear presentation of results and rationale for approval. That presentation is then followed by several days of questions and answers. Panel members ask about any aspect of the drug, and the CDO is expected to answer in detail. And he can, because he has an interactive slide library at his fingertips. No sooner does the AdComm expert ask a specific question about the chemical composition of the drug than the CDO can search and present the slide with detailed information and a diagram of the compound.

Maybe then another panel expert asks about the methodology of Phase II trials. The presenter can switch and quickly find and project slides about Phase II trials. As Steven Weisman, co-founder of ISS notes, "Speakers are always presenting in high-pressure situations that require them to think on their feet and retrieve content quickly when asked. One misstep can drastically lower the odds of approval – costing companies millions of dollars." Interactive presentations allow for back and forth, real discussion, between the presenter and the panel experts. The presenter can offer detailed, accurate information showing the AdComm that this drug has been properly developed, tested and is ready for market, while the AdComm gets the information it needs to recommend FDA approval.

The presentation follows the conversation.

Interactivity lets you manage the presentation *during* the meeting. It is more in line with how people think. Our minds are not linear. Even when we are focused on something, our minds still wander. Adjusting the meeting to your audience's wandering mindset will help you engage, educate and ultimately convince people to act, which is what presentations are really for -- incenting action.

Interactive meetings are more productive meetings. We learn how to better serve our clients and business partners when they are sharing their knowledge and concerns with us. When the presenter and the audience are both forcing themselves through a linear list of preconceived slides, it severely limits engagement, participation and feedback. Feedback is how we learn more about our clients' and colleagues' needs, so we can offer a better solution. The ability to adjust the content on-demand, during the meeting, and provide accurate information about a colleague's issue will push a sale or an FDA approval further along. The presenter doesn't have to say, "I'll get back to you on that," which will add weeks, even months to a deadline. Interactive presentations empower presenters to cover more, and do more, in the same amount of limited meeting time.

Interactive meetings elevate the presenter. When you answer your customers' issues on demand, you are perceived as smarter and more sincere. You are showing your customers that you are genuinely concerned with their problems, and you know how to solve them. In so doing, you elevate yourself from salesman to partner. Typically, CEOs and other senior-level executives can answer questions off the cuff. With interactive presentations, you are giving everyone in your company that ability. A junior sales rep looking for a deal can come across like a smart and trusted partner. Clients buy more from smart people whom they trust. Interactive meetings can positively affect your bottom line.

Better Storytelling

Stories are powerful for communicating, teaching, motivating and learning. That's because stories draw on emotion and scenarios that resonate with us on a visceral level. Better stories get people to act.

Presentations are stories for business. A good presentation tells a story about your business. It could be about the entire business or just one product. With your interactive slide library at your fingertips, you can tell a better story, based on your customer's immediate feedback, on the fly. You have the ability to present content that you know will appeal to your customer, and you can adjust the story as you learn more about your customer's situation. By creating a more relevant presentation, you are telling a better story.

The best presenters are great storytellers. They instinctively know how to draw their audience's emotions to engage them in their message. Presentation management can help all of us, even if we're not natural storytellers, to tell our company's story.

Back in 2003, this discipline helped Screenvision sell a new product, called Screenvision Premier, to an old industry of traditional advertising agencies. Screenvision Premier branded the movie theater. Sure, advertisers were willing to pay to project their ads on a big screen to play for a captive audience before the movie started. But what about the rest of the theater, like the lobby space where everyone milled about? Or the popcorn bags and soda cups? Screenvision had a means to brand all elements of the movie experience, but they had to sell it to advertisers. Imagine the media buyer's incredulous response to a junior Screenvision rep: "You want me to do what with a bag of popcorn?" Using 3-D imaging of the movie theater, complete with moviegoers walking around the lobby with branded bags of popcorn, the junior rep was able to communicate the value of this program. "Your product and logo look great on the popcorn bag that your customer will hold on his lap for 2½ hours."

The imagery helped tell the story of Screenvision Premier. It simplified the message and equipped the sales team to sell a new, novel idea.

In the pharmaceutical world, telling the AdComm about the patients who participated in a trial and how their condition improved -- complete with pictures and videos -- tells the human story of that drug's impact. The panel will not see the human element through a bunch of hard data, line graphs, charts and diagrams of molecules. The panelists need to understand the human element -- the emotion that moves people.

Presentation management makes great stories accessible to everyone, so whether or not you have the personality of a late-night talk show host -- and let's be honest, most of us do not -- you can still tell a story through a presentation that resonates and stirs the audience to act.

The Next Step: Making Presentations Intelligent

At first, presentation management might seem like it's taking PowerPoint and other files and putting them in a cloud with a few frills. But there's another aspect of presentations that comes alive once they are managed in a cloud environment where they can be tracked.

Presentations throw off data. Every word and pixel is data. Every time a slide gets used, the data can tell us who used it, and where and how it was used. The data can tie sales presentations, for instance, to deals closed, which means the data could show which slides helped sell the most product.

All of that data can be captured and analyzed in ways that help make every presentation better.
Presentation management tracks usage of files and slides in different scenarios. This provides a concrete understanding of what files, what messages and what products are being used and by whom.

Presentation management includes social tools for users in the field to give feedback in real time, associated with real content and activity. Users can comment and collaborate on files and slides through conversation threads, comments, likes, etc. in real time, spontaneously. It's like Facebook, except for marketing material instead of someone's vacation. (As Alex says: I know I'd rather look at sunsets on a sandy beach than last quarter's sales figures, too. But we need those sales to afford the beach vacation.)

The combination of data and anecdotes from the field provides a full picture of how the content is performing in the field, and where and how to make adjustments to your message and content as your business evolves.

Machine Learning and Modeling

Artificial Intelligence is about organizing enormous amounts of data, drawing conclusions and acting on them. The ubiquity of mobile technology has made it possible to collect millions of users' activity, then analyze and apply it to some purpose. For Amazon, this means suggesting products for you to buy based on what you purchased last month, and what you're browsing through today. For Google, it means finishing phrases, suggesting search terms based on what you just started to type into the search window, or based on what ads or articles you clicked on. These actions are tracked, and the data collected. The more actions are tracked, the more data gathered, the better AI can make "suggestions" or predict actions and behaviors. Then those actions are further tracked, analyzed and as a result, AI can fine-tune and improve. AI builds on itself, over generations of data.

This applies to presentations because presentations are no longer one-and-done lone files; they are enterprise assets. The same files are used and reused throughout many different scenarios, and results are collected, tracked and analyzed. It's the foundation for intelligent presentations -- what we call Predictive Slides™.

Predictive Slides will suggest which files and slides you should include in your new presentation based on who you are, to whom you are presenting and what you have presented in the past. During meetings, Predictive Slides will suggest slides based on how that conversation is progressing. This is the future of presentations, and we'll get into much more on that in the final chapter.

CHAPTER 3 - TAKEAWAYS

1. Components of presentation management include a central repository for storage and a slide library where users can find and reuse slides.
2. Active files are accessible, visualized and formatted to present. They are productive, working files.
3. Presentation management increases the ROI of your content creation.
4. Interactive presentations give presenters more flexibility during meetings and encourage audience members to participate. This makes for more productive meetings.
5. Presentations are the stories for your business.

6. Predictive Slides™ are the future of presentations.

CHAPTER 4

Culture of Presentation Management

Change is hard, especially in a large organization. People are afraid of the unknown. The *familiar* is our security blanket. Knowing where we will be and what we will be doing tomorrow makes us feel safe. Any effort to change that, especially in our jobs -- our livelihoods -- will be resisted.

Over the years, as we've worked with clients to launch their new presentation strategy, we've found that there are a few steps you can take to help your team embrace presentation management. Some of them are concrete, like training, and others are more psychological, like how to change someone's predisposition toward doing things a certain way. In this chapter, we will discuss the approaches you can take to lead your team into a presentation management culture. And it will also help you jump-start your presentation initiative.

Presentation management has two core tenants, and every step you take in your presentation management initiative should ultimately lead to those objectives. Revisit these tenants from time to time to make sure you stay on track.

1. Transform your presentations from one-and-done tactical files to enterprise assets.
2. Balance the long-term enterprise objectives and the individual needs of everyday employees.

The goal is to balance the presentation needs of both the individual and the enterprise

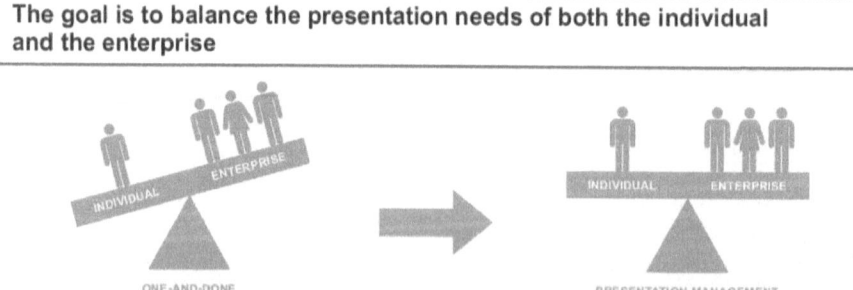

Director of Presentation Management

Presentation management is a disciplined approach to executing that strategy. The strategy guides who in your organization can present what message, to whom and when. It balances the objectives of the enterprise with the individual's needs. The approach is similar to any other marketing communications discipline, like advertising, public relations and event marketing. It has a similar process: define objectives, plan, execute, measure and then revise.

The director of presentation management, with the help of strategists, should spearhead your company's presentation management effort.

This person, or task force depending on the size and complexity of your company, should have an understanding of your company's messaging and branding. This role ensures that the presentation material is consistent with the company's mission. He should also have an understanding of the company's product and service lines to determine what kind of content to include in the library. Your presentation director should be a relatively senior executive who understands the business, its sub-divisions and has a sense of what the team members need to succeed in their roles. This is a role that probably already exists in your company. Someone or group, usually in marketing, has taken on this task by default because it's important.

Think of a museum curator who assembles the best collection of art. The presentation director is going to curate the best collection of your company's slides. He may source corporate communications to get the high-level content about the company. Then, to address the day-to-day presentation needs of individuals, the director can source content about specific products and services. In bigger companies, the presentation director usually delegates this task to managers from each division.

Cooper Standard, a global enterprise with over 100 locations across four continents, sourced content from each product line and region to create a comprehensive library. Get the content from the subject matter experts, wherever they are.

Once the content is collected, the director can organize the high-level corporate content with the detailed product content into one central cloud location. A presentation director is the curator of presentation content.

Promote the Benefits – It's PM for *Them*

Appeal to your employees' self-interest. Let your team know how presentation management will make their presentations better and easier. U.S. Bank surveyed its team members to understand their presentation pain points before choosing a solution. The bank found that, above all else, users really needed an easier way to find approved slides, so they wouldn't be forced to create their own. When the bank was ready to launch presentation management, management was able to communicate that this new presentation initiative would standardize content, push out slide updates and save time when preparing decks. That's what the users needed, so management led with their needs.

Show Them It's Familiar: "You Already Know How to Do This"

Once employees understand how presentation management makes their work-lives better, show them that it's already familiar. If you want your child to eat more fish, you don't serve her steamed sea bass with capers and onions in a spicy tomato sauce. You start with fish sticks, because fish sticks are pretty close to chicken fingers. And all kids like chicken fingers.

Draw similarities to what employees already know and do. For example, presenting in interactive mode, where they are pulling up slides on the fly, might seem intimidating. They lose the familiarity and structure of their linear PowerPoint. But they already tell stories through interactive presentation every day in their personal lives, especially if they're Millennials. Here's a familiar scenario that shows what we mean:

Suzanne and John are best buddies, but they haven't seen each other in a while. After rescheduling multiple times, they've finally caught up for dinner and drinks.

Standing at the bar, while waiting for their table John asks Suzanne, "How was your vacation?"

"Amazing!" Suzanne responds with delight. "We took the kids to Disney World. Funniest thing, my 4-year-old, Eric, has a huge crush on all of the Disney Princesses." She takes out her phone and starts scrolling through pictures. "Look at him blushing with Cinderella. Too cute! He's going to be mortified by this when he's older. And then we left the kids at my folks and hit the beach for few days to reboot." Suzanne shows a few more pictures of her and her husband enjoying a romantic dinner. "How about you?"

"I have a job interview in two days at Acme Company. It would be a promotion and raise. I'm so sick of my current job right now. I need to nail this."

"My friend used to work at Acme. Who are you meeting with?"

"Mike Whatshisface, he's the SVP of marketing," John replies. Suzanne starts the recon. She sends an inquiring text to her friend and does a Google search to get some more info on Mike Whatshisface. They both look at Suzanne's phone.

They pull up his LinkedIn profile and see that he started out in sales. Suzanne advises John, *"The guy has a sales background. Better talk about your experience in terms of results. You know, focus more on the results you've achieved and less about the process and details."* Then they go to Google images and find a picture of Mike Whatshisface and his wife at a charity event.

Meanwhile, Suzanne's friend replies to her text with a bitmoji of her running in fear, *"Mike Whatshisface is a total jerk. Tell John ... Run awaaaay!"*

They both break out in laughter and order another round of drinks.

That's an interactive story, using a mobile phone to present "slides" as the conversation unfolds. The content on your phone is formatted to present. Your phone is essentially a slide deck with the presentation following the conversation. When discussing interactive presentations, draw comparisons to what's already familiar.

Other aspects of presentation management should be familiar to most people, too. Your team already knows how to search and shop for stuff on Amazon, put pictures of items into a shopping cart and buy with one-click. Well, with a new presentation management initiative, employees are going to be able do the same thing, except with slides instead of items, which users will save into a new deck instead of to a shopping cart.

Training Starts the Conversation

Training provides a two-fold opportunity. First, it teaches the users how to use the new platform – click here, drag and drop there, etc. Second, training provides an opportunity to help your team embrace this new communication strategy called presentation management.

Cooper Standard is a world leader in automotive and aviation parts with over 30,000 employees. We developed a training program with them that covered the "how" and the "why" for presentation management, and included multiple touch points to reach such a diverse and geographically dispersed group.

Chris Andrews, the Director of Digital and Marketing Communications for Corporate Communications, and her marketing team of writers and designers created a library of branded, compliant presentations. For their presentation management launch, Andrews served as the presentation director and her team acted as the presentation task force. They started their slide library with high-level information about product lines, including sealing systems, fuel- and brake-delivery systems and fluid-transfer systems. They also included a slide about each facility. And then, the team started talking with their division and regional leaders about presentation management.

Here's how Andrews' team approached the task:

1. Training the influencers – Once Andrews and her team had a foundation for their library, they scheduled sessions with the regional leaders in North America, South America, Europe and Asia. Since the attendees were joining from four continents, Andrews' team conducted the sessions via web meeting. We showed them Shufflrr's features and functions, but more importantly, Andrews discussed why Cooper Standard was moving toward a presentation management platform, and how this new platform was going to make it easier and better for employees and partners to distribute and share accurate and branded slides all over the world. While the products may be the same, business protocols and cultures are very different from country to country. So, Andrews asked each attendee how he or she thought it would affect that region and how the system should be rolled out. For example, Asia required a different language and alphabet. So, we worked specifically with that director to tailor a separate training program for the Asia region. The meetings were less how-to tutorial and more conversation. Everyone participated.

2. Training the users – With such a dispersed group, our team at Shufflrr collaborated with Cooper Standard and created several means of training with different touch points. The first and, we believe, most impactful was in-person classroom training. We hosted several training sessions in different offices around Michigan, where Cooper Standard is headquartered. Those who could not physically attend could log in in through Webex. Andrews began these sessions with the reasons Cooper Standard launched a presentation management initiative. She explained to her colleagues that presentation management would make it much easier for them to assemble a presentation. She started each session by showing off all of the new content that her team had created, the library of polished, professional product and facility slides, the videos and other materials that were now so easy to find and use. She also emphasized that the slides in the library coincide with Cooper Standard's larger brand initiative. Users could get their jobs done and build the company's image. It balanced the enterprise marketing goals with the daily needs of employees. We then showed them how the system works. However, with every feature demonstration we gave a reason why that feature was important. We showed them how to receive a slide update, but we also explained that slide updating would ensure that they had the latest, branded version of that slide. Since Cooper Standard is continually innovating, slide updating is a feature users will want so they can keep up.

3. More web training – It's impossible to get everyone in the same room or on the same webinar. This is also true for smaller companies. We scheduled multiple sessions across several months to give everyone an opportunity to participate.

4. Ask for feedback – Andrews understood that training doesn't end with the session. It's easy to lose people's attention once they leave a meeting. Her team sent out a survey asking for feedback and suggestions on the presentation management program and the training sessions so we could improve as we continued. The request for feedback is a means to keep the conversation going.

5. Make it fun and rewarding -- Adoption is usage, and the marketing team needed to get their colleagues to embrace and start using the new presentation management solution. So, marketing created a contest. The game consisted of a series of exercises to complete in Shufflrr, using features and functions highlighted during training sessions. The catch is that they hid a slide in the library, the Golden Slide. As part of the game, aka practice exercises, users were asked to create a new presentation that included the Golden Slide and send it back to Andrews using Shufflrr's share feature. To play the game, they had to search, preview, drag and drop,

save a new presentation and share. They had to use and learn their tool's features. Those who completed the task got a prize. While playing the game, employees were learning how to use their new slide library. And they could win cool stuff.

6. <u>Training materials</u> – With the understanding that you will never get everyone with one program, Andrews provided her colleagues with how-to videos, long-form recording of live training, and cheat sheets. The idea is that anyone can reference any of these materials within their presentation management system when it's convenient for them.

Andrews and her team at Cooper Standard understood that training is an ongoing conversation. She did not expect a global team to change their habits and thinking around presentations after one 45-minute session. She also understood that it's not a one-way lecture. She engaged her colleagues, each group at their own level, and step-by-step, encouraged them to think differently about the role of Cooper Standard presentations within the company.

Launch in Phases

If your company is a large enterprise with 1,000-plus users dispersed over several different divisions, start small. Pick a subset -- one division and its content. First off, it makes content collection easier. You only have to collect and organize content for one product instead of 15. Second, a pilot team of 50 instead of 500 is much easier to manage. It gives you an opportunity to work out the kinks before going live to the entire organization.

When U.S. Bank started deploying presentation management, its objective was to implement the solution across the organization, for 1,000 users. But it started small, with 100 users, and progressively added content and users every month. The bank hosted regular training sessions for new users, and was able to accept feedback and make changes as it went along. Management created a cycle of add content, train, get feedback, adjust, add more content, train another group, get feedback, adjust, and keep going. It was a step-by-step process of managed growth. Through that process, the bank onboarded its goal of 1,000 users, and then got 500 additional requests to join the system. Word got out, and presentation management spread throughout the bank.

Collect Content

Your presentation management strategy is only as good as the content provided.

Systems, protocols, features, functions, cutting-edge technology and good intentions are all great. But content is king! Both U.S. Bank and Cooper Standard introduced slide libraries with the best content – branded, up to date, accurate, well-designed, well-written content. When word got out at U.S. Bank that there was a library that had all the good content, and all you had to do was drag and drop, requests for access increased and the presentation management mentality started to spread.

Content is how you balance the enterprise with the individual – the strategic with the tactical.

You can start from scratch and create all-new content. Luckily, that's not a requirement. Most of this content, enterprise and tactical, already exists. It's already saved on your network somewhere, embedded in other presentations, brochures, videos, etc. So it's a matter of identifying it and then including it in your presentation management initiative. The trick is to make sure that your presentation cloud includes both aspects of your business, the enterprise files and the tactical files, that can then be broken down into pieces where individuals can select and organize a new presentation for their own meeting.

Now you might be thinking something like, "You want me to parse through all of those files on our mess of network? Ugh!" Content collection may seem like a daunting task, arguably worse than spring cleaning. There are probably thousands of files on your network, so where do you start? It's really not as bad as it sounds. Big tasks are easier to accomplish when broken down into manageable chunks. There is no one-size-fits-all approach to content, but there are a couple of practical approaches we suggest when helping our own clients execute their presentation management strategy.

- The last 50
    - Sort through your network by date, and select the latest 50 presentations (or 100 or 30 or whatever number of files seems right for your organization), and other files that were created. This will give you the most up-to-date content to start with.
    - Review the files.
    - Delete redundant slides.

- Apply consistent brand standards, i.e., backgrounds, fonts, style, etc., to all files and slides.
- Organize them into smaller decks based on subject.
- Include high-level corporate information.
- Include product and service details.

* Delegate to divisions
    - Ask marketing managers from each division to contribute presentation content for their team. After all, they're the ones who are closest to their product messaging and to their presenters' needs.
    - Include corporate marketing and communications as their own divisions. They are great sources for enterprise content.
    - Review for duplication.
    - Delete redundant slides and content.
    - Apply consistent brand standards, i.e. backgrounds, fonts, style, etc., to all files and slides.

Users need slides and files to do their job. The goal of presentation management is to provide that tactical content to them in an easy, effective way. When your team sees compliant, productive content that they need to do their job within their presentation management solution, they will not just warm up to the new solution, they will embrace it. Remember when we talked about starting with "what's familiar." Well, your team is *very familiar* with the content they need to succeed in their job. Give them what they want.

CHAPTER 4 – TAKEAWAYS

1. Assign someone or group to own and direct your company's presentation management initiative.
2. Launch in phases. Add content in phases. And train in phases.
3. Start with what's familiar.
4. Training is like an ongoing conversation. Provide a range of training options and opportunities for your team to learn about and adapt presentation management.
5. Content is king! Give your team the content they need, formatted and ready to present, and they will embrace your new presentation management solution.

CHAPTER 5

Lifecyle of a Presentation

"Our presentations never finish," says Bob Davis, associate vice president of marketing for HealthTrust Purchasing Group, the purchasing division for HCA Healthcare, which operates 178 hospitals and 119 surgical centers throughout the United States and United Kingdom.

In presentation management, files are never "done." Instead, they evolve, just like the businesses they represent. Slides and decks continually morph and adjust to the market and to the world in which the business operates. The companies and organizations that get the most out of presentation management evolve their content through a constant lifecycle – or what we call *The Wheel*.

The Wheel looks like this:

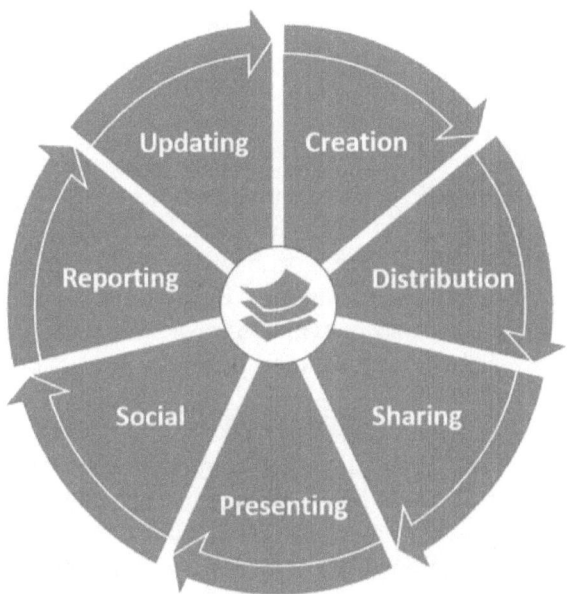

The process illustrated by The Wheel involves seven steps that generally follow each other, leading back to the beginning.

As we describe the elements in this chapter, you will notice that they overlap. In nature when something evolves there is no clearly defined start and end to a phase, but rather things morph. Same holds true for your presentation files. They morph from one phase to the next in the communication cycle of a corporate presentation.

The first step is creation – the act of creating slides and other content for presentations. Once created, the files are distributed through the presentation management system – into the cloud to be accessed by anyone with permission. Sharing goes hand-in-hand with distribution – in this case, sharing content with others inside or outside the enterprise.

Presenting is the act of using the content to present. Socializing the presentation is a way to get comments and feedback. Reporting means gathering data about how content is being used to better understand what's effective. Then all of that feedback and data can be used to update and improve slides and decks – a new act of creation that starts the process all over again.
Let's break down the details of each step.

Presentation Creation

In presentation management, creation means both content collection as well as the actual creation of a file.

A lot of good content probably already exists around your company. It's a matter of identifying the files, and then deciding if they are presentation management-worthy – for short, PMW. How do you determine if a file is PMW? Presentation management addresses both the long-term enterprise vision and the tactical day-to-day needs of employees. We suggest starting with the experts for each division. They most likely have great content for their particular product on hand.

Cooper Standard asked the regional leaders around the world as well as the directors for each product line. Each director made recommendations for how their content should be used, and then they contributed the content. As you review your company's content, ask yourself which files cover enterprise information, which files cover tactical information and which files cover both. What content is big picture? What content is going to get my sales rep to close the deal? Or move a project forward? Or educate a new hire? What are the team's objectives? That will determine which content is PMW.

Content can be created in any application. PowerPoint is the most obvious. Thirty million PowerPoint presentations get created every day.

PowerPoint is broken into individual slides, and each slide is a story in itself. PowerPoint makes it really easy to prepare presentations for those tactical, everyday meetings that keep the company humming along.

But presentation management doesn't have to be confined to PowerPoint. It can work with other apps. Apple's Keynote has great visuals and effects; Google Slides is cloud-based, which makes access easy; and Prezi is a popular app to create interactive presentations. Presentation management works with all file types that your team members use every day to get their job done: videos, images, Word docs, PDFs, spreadsheets, you name it. Make content in Photoshop, Quark, Apple iMovie -- it doesn't matter as long as the files can be previewed, reused and repurposed when needed. Anything that can be presented to and discussed with one or more people is content that should be considered in your presentation management strategy.

Compliance should go hand-in-hand with creation to make sure content is up-to-date, accurate, branded and approved. Your industry will determine your compliance requirements, which can be implemented and enforced through the presentation management platform. Here are a few examples of compliance:

- **Legal Compliance:** In highly regulated industries like health care and financial, strict rules govern what can be presented, to whom, by whom, in what format or context and finally with proper disclosures and disclaimers. Your PM strategy can manage this content in three ways. First, with routing and workflow approvals that ensure that the lawyers and regulators have approved the content before it becomes available to the team. Second, with file- or slide-locking features to prevent your team from changing text or other content. And third, by linking features to force required disclaimer and disclosure statements along with the content where appropriate. With presentation management you can force your dispersed team to present content in a very specific way – a way that complies with the law and reduces your company's risk of lawsuits and fines. Our banking clients used slide linking to match the proper disclosure statement to the corresponding slide.
- **Brand Compliance:** Brand compliance refers to brand guidelines, graphics, colors, fonts, logos and templates for all files that follow the brand's guidelines. The benefits are twofold. First, you achieve consistent branding across the enterprise. Second, because your employees are starting with higher-quality content, they appear more polished and professional, but they also become more productive. As they repurpose presentations, they can actually focus on the specifics of their project or deal instead of trying to

play graphic designer to make the slides look nice. We encourage all our clients to use only branded content. Start with the best.
- **Message Compliance:** What your employees say and how they say it are critical to your company's success. Message compliance ensures that your team is using the right language and the right version of the slide or file. It's achieved through good old-fashioned copywriting. And, like legal compliance, it can also be achieved through slide and file linking. For example, if a case study is five slides long, you can link all five slides, so if a user chooses one, he or she always gets all five. This way employees are forced to present the case study in its entirety, ensuring that they tell the whole story, and not just the bits and pieces that they like. (Imagine if we could do that in our personal lives. There would be no misunderstandings, no rumors or good gossip! And then we'd have nothing to talk about over cheap Chardonnay.)

Your presentation management strategy is as good as the presentation content provided. Collecting, creating and policing all of a company's content may seem like a big task, and it may very well be the first time around. But once that investment has been made, it will make everyone in your organization more productive, and the lifecycle will perpetuate itself as part of the normal course of business. It's a one-time investment that reaps exponential rewards.

Distribution

Where will the content reside? How will it be accessed? Who gets access? How do users find the specific content they need? Those are all issues concerning distribution in presentation management. Let's answer these questions one at a time.

Where is the content? Host the content on the cloud, because that's where users can get to it, whether they are sitting inside corporate headquarters or working from home. Most of our clients subscribe to our hosting service. But there are a few who prefer to keep their content on the premises, in which case they install Shufflrr on their own cloud. The goal is to make sure users can get content, anywhere, anytime, from any device. There's nothing more frustrating than sitting down at your desk to get some work done only to realize that you are locked out for some dumb reason.

How is content accessed? Access begins with logging into the slide library. Users then find content through search and visualization. The quality of the slide library, visualization, content hierarchy, search and permissions will affect the ease or the difficulty with which users can successfully find what they need.

What about logins? The No. 1 reason we get help requests: a user can't log in, usually because he or she forgot the password or URL. It happens all of the time for cloud services, not just for Shufflrr. Most of our clients support single sign-on, or SSO. When a user is logged into the company network, he or she can access the library. There are no additional passwords to remember. To make it even easier, some clients create a dashboard of all of their services on one home page. That way employees don't need to remember a bunch of different URLs. The benefit of SSO is that when employees leave the company, they lose access to their slide library, too. From a security standpoint, it's tighter. Another option is to integrate your presentation management solution with a complementary content management system (CMS) like Box or SharePoint, or a sales enablement service like Salesforce. Last, but not least, a login can be a stand-alone with unique credentials. Choose the path of least resistance, whatever will be easiest for your team to find and access their slide library.

How does the visual slide library work? All files in presentation management are formatted and ready to present. A slide library is a tool that visualizes the content. It makes a thumbnail of every slide in a PowerPoint or page in a Word doc. You can give content a quick preview, or read it closely, so you can decide if it's the right content for your next meeting. Then you can select the pieces of those files and reorganize them into your new presentation. The purpose of the slide library is to turn every piece of content into a slide, ready for use. The slides are then presented to the user so he or she can decide to use it in a new presentation. Like it's saying, "Look at me! I have some great words, with nice animations and a pretty picture. Pick me for your new presentation!" A piece of content can also say, "Present me right now in the middle of your meeting. I've got all the info your client is asking about, and I am ready to go." That's an accessible slide library with productive content.

What is content hierarchy? This is how the content is organized. It's a combination of folders, subfolders and tags. A good place to start when trying to decide how to organize your content is to look at how your company is organized: by product, by service, by region, etc. For example, pharmaceuticals organize their content by drug and disease. Financial services companies usually organize their slide library by banking service: retail banking, wealth management, business banking, etc. International cruise lines organize their content by tour destinations and ships. Also consider the purpose of the content: case studies, company histories, product overviews and executive bios all serve different objectives. The objective of a piece of content will determine where to put it in the hierarchy and who will be given access.

Content hierarchy is integral to presentation strategy. Your presentation management team will ask what is the content, who will present it, and in what business setting. The answers to those questions will guide the content hierarchy for your library, and guide the permissions.

How does the search function operate? No matter how well-structured that hierarchy is, everyone's thought process is different. Think of a 10-year-old boy looking for his socks. He calls down to his mother, "Mom, where are my socks?" She replies, "In your room, where they belong." She's thinking the dresser. But the poor child is looking on the floor because that's where little boys think all things should go, including socks. Two different perspectives in the same place, for the same item. And that's why a visual search tool is critical for distribution. Visual search lets you preview thumbnails of the search results, so you can skim through your options before you make a choice. Contextual search, where the files are automatically indexed upon inclusion in your slide library, will minimize the need for additional meta-tags, and compensate for content hierarchy limitations. Contextual search means that all of the text that occurs naturally within the file: the file name, the titles and subtitles, the body copy and for PowerPoint speaker notes, is automatically searchable. Filtering search parameters allows users to zoom into a subset of content. When you have a library of 1,000 files and 10,000 slides, the ability to set your own search parameters will save users a lot time wasted browsing through the wrong files. In presentation management, we just want to make sure that everyone and anyone can find the files they need. Advanced search tools help achieve that.

Metadata, which is just a fancy word for tags, are another tool for organizing and searching for content. If a word naturally occurs within the context of the copy, then you don't need to tag it. It will show up in the search. Add tags to a slide or file when it won't naturally show up in search. Tags can also provide another way to organize the content. Tag a hundred files, and when the user does a search against that one tag, a clean list of files will appear.

What about permissions? Permissions are a critical element of distribution because they direct the right content to the individuals and groups who need it most. And permissions hide content from people who should not use it. We wouldn't want to burden a research assistant with financial content, for instance.

Permissions are a matrix of content access and functionality: who gets access to which files, and what are they allowed to do with those files. The answers to the questions below will be different for different members of your team. For example, an end-user in the field will have fewer editing permissions than a brand manager who is responsible for creating and updating her team's content. Most of our clients create groups of users with the same permissions. The groups, like the content structure, represent the different lines of business, regions or executive levels in the company.

Here are some permissions that can be granted or denied. When applied to your organization, permissions allow for control of the message and mitigate risk caused by misuse of content. "They" in this case refers to individuals and groups. "They" will have a different permission level depending on who they are, and what they need to accomplish.

Can they see it?	
Can they use the content, as is?	
Can they download it, remove it from the system?	
Can they download it in editable format?	
Can they download it in a locked or PDF format to prevent editing?	
Can they edit content?	
Can they contribute content?	
Can they organize the content into a hierarchy for their colleagues?	
Can they force those edits on other users?	
Can they mix and match that file with other files?	
Can they give other company users access to it?	
Can they share it with a third party?	
Can they make comments on a piece of content, a file or slide or video?	
Can they "like" or rate the content?	
Can they see and configure reports?	
Can they grant or deny permissions?	

Distribution is ultimately about productivity with control of the content, who is using it, and how they are using it. The purpose of control is to reduce risk and ensure consistent, accurate messaging across your organization.

Sharing

Sharing refers to how you share or send files to your clients and other third parties outside of your organization. This is especially important for sales, marketing and investor relations. Those presentations directly affect the company's image and bottom line. It's a seemingly mundane task, but it has huge implications for productivity. Files with images and videos tend to get too large and will be stripped from most corporate email systems. The file-size limit is different for every organization, so you don't really know if your file will get through or not. Sharing gives media ad sales reps an easy way to send large video files to advertisers. Travel clients have high-resolution pictures and videos in their presentations, too. Anyone in any industry can have big files. The process of sharing these presentations is simple: Choose one or more files. They could be large PDFs, PowerPoints, Images or Videos, it doesn't matter, as long as they tell the right story. Click on "Share," input your customer's email address and within seconds your customer can view the files. Like YouTube. It's instantaneous.

Then, you can track consumption of the files. Did my client open it, download it, read it, ignore it -- or maybe she just never received it? It's productive to know how engaged your client is with the information you share because that will tell you how interested they are, and then help guide your next steps.

Similar to the permissions we just discussed, the shared files have permissions as well – permission to download, to edit, to view only and whether that would be for a limited time frame or in perpetuity. Users not only track how their recipients are consuming the files they send, they can also control their usage.

Share usage is a component in reporting. One user can track his shares for his own purposes, and the team leaders, which might be the presentation director and the VP of sales, can analyze share data for all users across the enterprise. Managers can see patterns and trends in content sharing, and make content adjustments accordingly.

Presenting

It wouldn't be presentation management without *the presenting*. With today's technology there are many options for how you present your content.

Human contact is how relationships are solidified. Look people in the eyes, read their body language, watch them react to what you are saying. That is how strong relationships are built. Presentation management fosters better business relationships through higher-quality meetings. Let's look at how in some different presentation settings.

One-to-one: One-to-one meetings are less formal and more intimate. The presenter can give the presentation directly from her laptop, iPad or even her phone. One-to-one presentations allow for more feedback and discussion. It's also an easier format to switch to interactive mode, where the presenter selects content based on the other person's feedback. The presentation can follow the conversation. The presenter can learn more and therefore propose a better solution tailored to that person. These are very productive meetings.

One-to-several: This is typically a conference room setting where one presenter is addressing a group of up to 20 people. A monitor or screen is needed. Though it's more formal in nature, there is still the opportunity to go interactive as audience members raise issues and ask questions. The FDA Advisory Committee presentations are one to several, with an emphasis on interactivity to conduct a detailed question and answer.

One-to-many: This is an auditorium setting, which is more formal. Presentation management allows the presenter to give a pre-rehearsed presentation while fielding and answering questions from audience members. The ability to answer tough questions on the fly, supported by visuals, adds to the speaker's credibility.

Conference: Slide libraries are an integral tool for conference managers who need to collect and manage presentations for any number of speakers. In this scenario, your presentation management solution will manage the collection, organization, approvals and presentations on the day of the event. It reduces the administration burden on the event managers. Speakers send a presentation directly to the slide library, where it is automatically tagged based on pre-configured speaker credentials. Workflow settings can be applied so the presentation gets routed to the appropriate editors and/or approvers in preparation for the conference. And finally, on conference day, the presentations are already tagged and sorted so they can be assigned to the appropriate speaker, breakout room and time. The presentation is right there, ready to go on the podium. The speaker can even present directly from the library, if your library has broadcast capability.

Linear versus interactive presentations: A linear presentation, like your typical PowerPoint, is a pre-ordered set of slides -- slide one, slide two, slide three, slide four and on and on.. It's organized, predictable and easy for the speaker to control. Interactive presentations are more like browsing a website: You click on one thing, which leads you to another. Then, someone asks a question, so you spontaneously pull up another slide, video or image that addresses that question. It's free-form and it follows the conversation. Linear presentations force the conversation. Interactive presentations follow the conversation.

Interactive presentations foster productive conversations where both sides learn more about the other. In more than 20 years of presentation consulting, we've noticed that the more senior the executive, the more likely they are to present in interactive mode. They don't need the security of a linear list. Though the nice thing about today's interactive presentation tools is that they can accommodate both scenarios. They can let you go off-topic and spontaneously present content, and then click a back button to get back to the main storyline. It's the best of both worlds: control and spontaneity.

Social
"PowerPoint is going social!" Kristin Shevis, Chief Customer Officer for Clarifai, exclaimed when we explained the social capability of our Shufflrr app. It's like Facebook or Instagram except the subject matter is your presentation content instead of your vacation pictures. (Yeah, I know, I'd prefer to see sandy beaches over org charts any day.) Users can follow, like, rate, comment and converse about files and slides.

Social provides spontaneous feedback in The Wheel, helping to improve the content's quality for its next evolution. When you are collaborating with colleagues, you can see their comments directly on the slide or the file they affect, and then you can respond. Permissioned users can also see the conversation thread, so everyone can understand the context of the file and see how and why it evolved to its latest iteration. On an enterprise level, users can give direct feedback to their presentation team about the content in real time. They can write a quick comment about what's good on a slide, or bad, or how a client reacted in a meeting given 15 minutes ago. It helps the presentation director asses the quality of the content, what's resonating in the field and why, and provides direction for edits and updates going forward. Social also provides a means to give input and share knowledge among the entire group, rather than waiting for that next big status meeting. And let's be honest, by the time that status meeting comes around, you've forgotten about that slide anyway. That's why presentation management has commenting and other social features built in, to keep the feedback loop continual and timely.

Reporting

Reporting makes presentations smarter. It gives you real intelligence about what's working and what's not. Data can be tracked across multiple variables: slide, file, user, group, time frame and action. Actions are whatever you can do with a slide or file, such as upload, download, delete, update, view, share, broadcast, comment, like, rate, etc. You name it, it's all tracked and time-stamped. Then, you can customize reports against any of these variables.

The reporting gives you real information that against which you can make real decisions. It helps determine what files and slides are used most often, by whom and presented to whom. What are your most popular products? What messages have your clients been exposed to? And what have they actually purchased? From there you can determine best practices and encourage those practices across other members of your team.

Charter Communications used reporting to cut the fat. The presentation team used to create brochures, rate cards and long-form decks for every single business category across 91 local markets. When the presentation team looked at their usage reports, they learned that their team of 1,500 reps barely used any of that content. They were successful without it. As a result, the presentation team cut down the material they created to just one three-slide deck for each category. They stopped wasting time and money creating content that wasn't needed. And the reps got a smaller, better-organized, library of content that was easier for them to search through.

The value of feedback in presentation management multiplies when the quantitative data in reports is combined with the qualitative feedback from social. A data log will tell you that a file was never used. But a comment from a user will tell you that the slide is butt ugly, and they are embarrassed to show it. The product wasn't bad, just the messaging. And now you know how to fix that slide, and give your team better content. Feedback and analytics give a current and ongoing view of your marketplace.

And that brings us to…

Updating

Now that you have all of this great information about what products and content need to change, it's useful and efficient to make the change once, and know that everyone in your organization will receive the updated version. It also helps to retire old, out-of-date, discontinued content. Ever sit in a meeting where your colleague pulls up last year's pricing? Or worse, products that your company no longer sells? I guess he didn't get the memo. With enterprise updating, you don't need a memo. It just happens, automatically.

As Bob Davis of HealthTrust Purchasing Group notes, "We are always rewriting. Our account directors come back from a meeting with feedback and suggestions, and we go right back and rewrite the slides. We are always working on our slides." With slide updating, he doesn't worry that someone is using an older, outdated, wrong version.

With slide updating, there is a genealogy that occurs in presentations. One parent presentation begets children. When a slide is reused, dragged and dropped into a newly created presentation, that new presentation becomes a child. At U.S. Bank, one parent slide can exist in over 300 different presentations across the company. When the presentation director in the home office updates that one parent slide, all 300 versions get updated as well. That's efficient, productive, compliant and consistent messaging.

The easiest way to incent a change is to start with what's familiar. The elements of presentation management are already familiar. We all know how to edit and create decks. Some of us are better at it than others, but in business, we've all made at least one presentation. We all know how to search through a network or a website to find content. Visualization and better search take the frustration out of that process. We share files on YouTube, Dropbox, and a million other formats all the time. That's nothing new. In business, we give presentations every day; the elements of presentation management make them better presentations. We spend hours commenting and liking on social media, so it's not a stretch to do the same with your presentation content.

And finally, in the age of big data, we rely on metrics to see what's trending so we make smarter decisions going forward. The elements of presentation management are not new, but presentation management is a new approach to how we treat our content and value presentations as an enterprise marketing asset.

CHAPTER 5 - TAKEAWAYS

1. Presentations evolve along with your business.
2. Presentation management is a comprehensive approach that facilitates each stage in the lifecycle of a presentation.
3. The stages in the life of a presentations are: creation, distribution, sharing, presenting, social, reporting and updating.
4. Content organization and search capability are critical elements to help your users actually find the content they need.
5. Reporting will not only track who is using which content, it guide better content and messaging decisions going forward.

CHAPTER 6

Making Better Presentations; Telling Better Stories

We like the phrase, "Content is king!" Without quality content, any presentation management implementation is a bit of waste.

When we started working with clients back in the '90s, every new job was a consulting project that including writing and designing presentations. Those presentation services were initially our primary source of income. We've worked with clients in every industry to help them write their stories and create libraries of slides that can be used and repurposed.

In this chapter, we will share what we've learned over the years about how to create exceptional presentations, including what we've learned from experts about how presentations effect the brains of those on the receiving end.

Presentations Are the Stories for Business

The best presenters are great storytellers. The CEO is often the best storyteller in the company. Motivating people to act is integral to her and the company's success, and stories do that better than statistics. Salespeople tend to be good storytellers as well, since their success is directly related to their ability to connect with customers. But employees in every department and function need to be good presenters. A research scientist can present a bunch of numbers with charts and graphs, and bore everyone to tears. But a great research presentation will tell the story of what that research means on a human level, with relatable characters and real feelings. That's more interesting and more memorable.

Imagine a Federal Express presentation to see what we mean. The FedEx company story is not just about the logistical genius of strategically placed shipping hubs combined with a fleet of trucks, cargo planes and ships, and a workforce of 250,000 delivery experts. Those are certainly elements that make the company successful. But the corporate story is about helping businesses succeed. Think of a hardworking executive under pressure to meet a deadline. The executive is tired, stressed and fearful of failure – of losing a client and losing her job because she might not deliver. All are strong emotions that we can relate to. Using FedEx, she can work until 9 p.m. and still get her product delivered to her client by 9 a.m. the next day. She gets more time to work, and her client is pleased to have the product on time. The sale gets closed. Everyone is happy. For this FedEx presentation, you could use images of stressed executives and combine them with facts about FedEx's locations and guarantees of timeliness. But you will remember that the executive was able to turn a harrowing situation into a success story.

So let's make the business world a better place, one presentation – one story – at a time. Here are some tips to help you craft better business stories, and then organize them in your presentation management solution so that your team can repurpose the slides and decks for their individual meetings.

Make It Relevant. Ask So What?
Every piece of content created should answer the question, "So what?" Whether you're creating one slide, an entire presentation, a brochure, an email or even a tweet, it should tell the audience why that point is important -- and, especially, why it's important to the intended target. It will take you out of your own head and put you in your audience's frame of mind. That mental exercise will push you to create more compelling content.

Here are a few messages that stand alone.

> *Our sales increased 15 percent.*
> *Our widgets were rated No. 1 by this prestigious industry organization.*
> *You are a jerk.*

Now let's take those three statements and add "So What?"

> *Our sales increased by 15 percent, which means you will get a bonus at Christmas.*
> *Our widgets were No. 1, which means you will get the best product for the lowest price.*
> *You are a jerk, which means no one wants work with you, and your job is in jeopardy.*

We want to know, what's in it for me? When you're writing a presentation, you want to flat-out tell your audience why this is important, and why they should care. Don't expect them to make that connection on their own. As a passive listener, that's not their job.

Rather, it's your job as an active communicator. *So what?* gives the audience relevance and motivation. Since the purpose of most business presentations is to get people to act, then better presentations provide really good reasons to do so. *So what?* gives them that reason.

Keep It Short. The 10-Minute Rule.

Our brains are lazy. According to molecular biologist John Medina in his 2008 book *Brain Rules*, the mind gets bored at 10 minutes. Next time you are in a not-too-exciting meeting -- ergo, the typical corporate meeting with a PowerPoint presentation -- check yourself when you check the time. It will be in 10 minutes.

A lot of our clients have very complicated products and services, and the story they need to tell cannot be told in a mere 10 minutes. Pharmaceutical companies have presentations that encompass everything about a drug: its molecular composition, uses, diseases it treats, clinical trials methodology and results, risks, legal disclosures and other information. Those presentations can grow to well over 100 slides. So what do you do?

To paraphrase Steve Jobs, do something big. His presentations were 30 minutes to an hour long. But every 10 minutes he'd break up the monotony by, say, introducing a new speaker, using a prop, or cutting to video. He broke up the monotony to keep listeners riveted.

Break up your presentation into 10-minute chunks. After 10 minutes, make a change. Switch presenters, introduce a prop, ask the audience a question. Do something to break up the monotony. When you have a very long presentation, break it down into sections and make an obvious change to re-engage your audience.

Make It Memorable

Have you ever walked out of a presentation with a phrase or image emblazoned on your mind? Or more likely, you've walked out of a presentation and couldn't recall a single thing. In one ear, out the other. Our presentations are competing with a million other things for our audience's attention, from email to mass media to family issues. Everyone is multitasking and distracted. Therefore, as presenters we have to work harder to not only get our message across but to make it memorable. We asked Carmen Simon, author of, ***Impossible to Ignore***, how to make memorable, impactful presentations.

Here's her advice.

1. Know what you want your presentation to be remembered for.
Determine what your audience should remember and why it is important. A lot of business communicators aspire to be memorable, but few know what specific memories they want to set in other people's brains. Audiences forget 90 percent of what you share after 48 hours. Pick the one thing that you really want your audience to remember, and reinforce it throughout your presentation.

2. Provide cognitive ease. Once it's clear to you what message you want to stick with your audience, make sure that message comes to their minds easily. Often we get enamored with our own words and ideas, and we forget that just because these messages come to our minds easily, they might not have the same effect on others. Here's an example. Carmen was sitting in a hotel lobby browsing through a magazine article about the new McLaren 570S Spider model. The main message focused on its "dihedral synchro-helix actuation," which is the technical term for the way the doors swing, guiding air into the side intakes to feed the radiators. Would you remember this phrase after two days? Dihedral-what? You might remember it if you were a car fanatic and might have existing mental models around this type of verbiage. For the average person, if we describe the doors as "up-and-out" doors or "butterfly doors," it will be easier to remember the message. Once you clarify the message you want to make memorable, ensure that the language you use makes the message come to others' brains easily. Cognitive ease is a prerequisite to memorable stories. Make it simple.

3. Use sensory stimulation. In the paragraph above, was it easier for you to process the phrase "butterfly doors" more so than other phrases? Visuals are important to memory because we build our memories through our senses, and visual is a powerful sense. Have you ever looked at a picture of a chocolate lava cake oozing fudge, and thought, I can almost taste it. That's because the visual image evokes your sense of smell, taste and chocolate satisfaction. It stimulates your senses. Appealing to other senses activates additional brain parts, which forms more memory traces. A presentation about arthritis could use a sensory description of arthritic pain like this: "knuckles cracking, throbbing and swollen so badly that she couldn't even hold her fork at dinner." Those words "throbbing" and "swollen" evoke pain, and using a fork at dinner is something we do every day, without a second thought (until we can't anymore).

The examples activate more brain areas (visual cortex, motor cortex, amygdala, frontal cortex, hippocampus). When more brain parts become active, it increases the chance that the stimuli you mention will trigger memories later on. Just in these few paragraphs, words such as doors, butterfly, pain, hands, dinner fork ... seeing any of these later may remind you of reading this. In short, try to evoke real human feelings.

How to Create a Story for Business – Formatted to Present

One of the elements of presentation management is that all content is visual, in slide format. Whether it's an actual PowerPoint slide, a four-page brochure, a white paper or a video, all the content is ready for presentation on a screen. When you write your next presentation, which is synonymous with telling your business story, think of story elements from a visual perspective. In presentation management, that's your end game. That means you need to think about content in a different way – a visual way.

PowerPoint is an outline. Typically, you open up PowerPoint and start typing in slides – a headline and some bullet points. When you write a presentation today, you are really just filling in an outline. To create better business stories, get out of outline mode and get into story mode. Here is a five-step approach to help you create better presentations by penning stories that engage your audience and tap into their emotions. We are using PowerPoint as an example because that's what most people use to create presentations. But you can apply these principles to any medium.

1. **Close PowerPoint.** Don't start creating a presentation by opening PowerPoint and filling in slides. Instead, figure out your story as if you were talking to someone about it over coffee. Once you've come up with a good story, track down someone — a colleague, a spouse or a friend — and practice telling them the story to see what they have to say. This forces you out of outline mode, and ensures that you're able to whittle the story down to the essentials that can impact the audience.

2. **Imagine a three-act play.** Every good story has a setup, climax and resolution -- a beginning, middle and end.

    - Setup: Establish the characters and the setting. In business, the characters are the products or services you are selling, or the objective of the task or project you are planning. The hero is the main driver of your presentation. The setting is your marketplace, situation or use case. It's the environment or the world in which your hero operates. Describe the hero, his situation, and why the hero is important to your audience.

- Climax: A good setup will lead the audience right into the big problem or obstacle to overcome. For a business presentation, this would be the pain points, market analysis, product challenges or failures and successes.

- Resolution: This is the happy ending — a problem solved, a product sold, a project completed. The outcome should feel meaningful, for everyone in your audience. It should answer the question, "So what?"

3. **Ask yourself how your story feels.** Emotions drive behavior more than logic. (Our friends in the ad business live by this, but the rest of us in the corporate world tend to forget it.) As noted in the previous section, we get so mired in our own intellectual ideas that we forget about the sensory aspect. Attach the corresponding emotions to the *So what?* points in your deck. While you want your stories to connect to your audience's emotions, you need to make sure that you're tapping into those emotions in a proper way. If you tap into the right emotions, you'll ultimately get them to "act" the way you want.

4. **Visualize the emotions.** What do these emotions "look" like? Once you have a handle on how your story feels, it's time to visualize the content. Match the image to the emotion and use descriptions and/or images that trigger the senses and activate the brain. Just keep in mind that whatever visuals and emotions you choose, you are supporting your story and moving it forward.

5. **Now, open PowerPoint and fill in your slides.** You have the story, you have the motivating emotions, and you have the triggers to make it memorable. The hard work, the thinking part, is done. PowerPoint is merely a conduit to communicate that story. It does not drive your story. The story will drive the slides – words, images, charts and videos.

Every presentation is a story. Every slide is a scene.
We went through five steps to create a great presentation. But if you've been following the principles of presentation management, by now you understand that presentations are corporate assets with long-term value – not just one-and-done.

So how do you take the principles of good storytelling, combined with visualization, emotion and sensory stimulation, and create presentations that any employee can take apart and repurpose for his or her own use? After all, in a large organization, a lot of different people are making presentations with different purposes. Every presentation could very well have a different beginning, middle and end. It's not one-size-fits-all. We want to empower everyone to be able to create great stories with the library of slides provided.

Make sure every slide is a scene in the bigger story. Each slide should be able to stand on its own. Think of a slide as its own subplot within the story. That way, when your team starts mixing the slides in ways that you never dreamed of, they will still create a professional, branded presentation that's on message.

Content Organization

The next step is to organize slides into a library that tells an even bigger story: the story of your enterprise. Apply the same methodology of "every slide is a scene; every presentation is a story" to your enterprise. If you work for a large enterprise, there are probably many departments divided by discipline, product or geography. Each department has a story. Here's how we built a presentation management solution for cable TV company Scripps Networks, which had a mission to improve their viewers' lifestyle and community. Its portfolio of networks included brands like Food Network, HGTV, DIY Network, Cooking Channel, Travel Channel and Great American Country. Each network answered a *So what?* that mattered to viewers. Furthermore, each program, each slide, had a more specific *So what?* that mattered to a particular demographic. For example, Rachel Ray showed people how to cook a great meal in 30 minutes, so we can eat well even when we don't think we have the time. That was important to time-strapped parents who worked outside the home. We organized content into chapters for each network and slides for each program. Each network told its overarching story: why it exists, what it means to the viewers and the value for advertisers and cable operators.

Then each program did the same, but on a smaller scale. The stories included factual information about the programs and their ratings, and also a human element about viewers and how that program changed people's lives. Each slide or set of slides told its own story. We didn't just create a chart comparing audience delivery of women 25 to 54 years old -- we stated why women 25 to 54 are such a lucrative target for advertisers, and included pictures and videos to bring that audience to life. The slides showed real people with real emotions who were affected by those programs. Even though it might be safe to assume that the advertisers in the room knew their target, Scripps went the extra mile and reminded them why their target is important. Finally, to keep the audience engaged, Scripps introduced different presenters to present the different networks, each with his or her own personality and character. And, the presenters broke up the slides with videos. The changes added energy to the Upfront roadshow presentations room and kept the meetings flowing. In doing so, Scripps demonstrated that it intrinsically understood the marketplace and how it affected its advertisers' business.

This approach "allowed all of our salespeople to speak intelligently, whether talking about the details of one program or the value of working with Scripps in general," said Jon Steinlauf, who was at that time, in 2005, Senior Vice President of ad sales for Scripps Networks. (He is now Chief Advertising Officer at Discovery Communications.) "Presentation management gave them the ability to cross-sell the networks, which translated into higher revenues."

In the Scripps library, each piece of content met the criteria for a good presentation management strategy. It was formatted to present; it told a relevant, memorable story; and it was branded and compliant. The 150 Scripps ad sales reps had a range of stories that they could repurpose and customize for their individual meetings. Because they were telling better stories, they became better presenters, and ultimately better brand stewards for Scripps.

CHAPTER 6 - TAKEAWAYS

1. Presentations are stories for business and every slide is a scene.
2. An effective presentation is memorable, relevant and short.
3. Memorable presentations appeal to multiple senses –physical and emotional.

4. Presentations, like good stories, should include a set-up, climax and resolution.
5. Get out of outline mode and into story mode. Develop your story, your presentation, in your head *before* you open PowerPoint or another program. Tell it to someone, imagine how it looks, and then you can start typing.

CHAPTER 7

The Future of Presentations

If you think about it, over the past century humans have been forced to adapt to technology and the structure it creates. It's not "normal" to work from 9 a.m. to 5 p.m. or write by typing on a QWERTY keyboard. Presentations are another example. We create linear slide decks, then conform our work conversations to the deck because that's the way the technology works, by showing us one slide at a time, in order. It's not the way we'd naturally talk and discuss a topic, but if we want to use technology, we have to do it technology's way.

In this century, technology is increasingly conforming to the way humans do things. Like, we can *talk* to our devices instead of tapping on a tiny screen. Presentations are moving that way, too. In fact, it is the biggest change in the nature of business presentations since the advent of PowerPoint. For the first time, the technology and the linear presentation deck will no longer dictate the conversation and interaction.

Instead, the conversation will dictate the presentation. Thanks to voice recognition and artificial intelligence, the next generation of presentation technology will listen to what's being said, comprehend the context in the room, know what visual content is available in the approved presentation management system, and automatically and instantly bring up visuals that fit the conversation at that moment. It's almost like having a personal assistant at your side, listening and watching the room, and instantly finding and showing images that are exactly what's needed in the moment.

How would technology like that work in practice? Imagine this scenario:

The CEO of a major cruise line is speaking at a travel conference in an auditorium that only seats 100 people. He cues up his presentation management app and it projects on the big screen and a few monitors inside the auditorium, as well as outside in the hallway and all around the convention center. Anyone who sees it, either sitting in the live audience, walking by one of those monitors, or browsing on a website, can participate in his presentation. They can log in to the presentation on their own phone or other device. After all, they have full A/V on their phone, where they can hear his presentation and see his slides. Someone in the audience raises his hand and asks a question that everyone in the audience, whether they are physically sitting in the auditorium or have logged in from 1,000 miles away, can hear. "Can you tell me more about cruises to Alaska?" As the voice-recognition technology processes the words in the question, AI starts to sort through the speaker's presentation library, which includes all content about the cruise line, including approved databases. Up pops slides with visual support for the question. The audience will see pictures of the Kenai Fjords, snow-capped mountains and a luxurious cruise ship, with every pampering amenity you could imagine, sailing through it all. It's conversational AI broadcast to the entire world.

Presentations will become more dynamic, more fluid, more like the human thought process. And the technology we use for presentations will become an afterthought.

And this is right around the corner – the way presentations will be within a few years. Voice-recognition technology is exploding. By 2020, it is estimated that over half of all searches will be powered by speech instead of keyboard input, according to comScore. That means that during an interactive presentation, the technology can listen to the audience's comments and questions. Those questions and comments will prompt a search. Suggestions for slides to present will appear based on the conversation as it unfolds.

That technology will expand with Predictive Slides™. Your presentation management app will offer slide suggestions based on a range of variables, such as who you are, the last slides you used, the slides your colleagues used, the audience, the most popular slides, and on and on. Companies will be able to customize those variables based on the individual user, and the presentation will be created based on those inputs and variables. It's similar to how shopping on Amazon works. Amazon presents products based your purchase and browsing history. Your presentation management app will present slides in a similar way.

This will also work at the slide level. Based on the user's input and criteria, slides will pull information from different databases to create a specific slide for one specific instance. For example, a financial adviser is meeting with his client. Today, he searches several different databases to review that client's portfolio, credit card debt, stock positions and IRAs, as well as age, income and stated financial goals. With all that information culled together, the adviser will then input that into another database to get suggestions for changes to the portfolio. And then, the adviser, or his admin, will create a nice slideshow. That's labor-intensive and prone to lots of human errors. In the future all of this data will feed directly into a formatted, branded slide ... visualized and ready to present.

Predictive Slides™ can be generated before the meeting or during the meeting, as the conversation progresses.

During the meeting, the slides themselves will be created according to verbal inputs based on what people are saying. Imagine the financial adviser is meeting with that client for the first time. He discusses the client's current financial status, her salary, her credit cards, mortgage, age, expenses and goals for her retirement. As the client speaks, the presentation app is accessing various financial databases to build her portfolio and then creates the slides on the fly. The adviser and the client review the presentation together. The operative word in this is scenario is *together*. The adviser is not presenting to, or talking at, the client. He's discussing the financial plan with her. She's responding, and the presentation is updating according to her immediate feedback. So the adviser can focus on the client, not the slides. The slides fall to the background while the two parties make a human connection, fostering trust and building a better relationship. They learn more about each other. The adviser not only gets a better understanding of his client's financial goals, which is the purpose of the meeting, but also of her personal life, which certainly affects her finances.

In the process, the client starts to trust her adviser and starts to see him as someone genuinely interested in helping her achieve her financial goals. After all, that's what usually happens when you break down barriers and just start talking with someone. As a result, the adviser is in a better position to help his client, because he knows more about her, and the client gets a better financial plan. It may sound ironic, but presentation technology will encourage human connection.

Advances in technology will free us from the very technology to which we've become so addicted. Hardware continues to get smaller and cheaper. You will be able to access your presentations from your phone, your watch and maybe even your glasses. Smaller devices will become ubiquitous, and as that happens they will also fall into the background. A watch is an accessory, it's not the outfit. Look around today and you'll see most people glued to a screen, clicking, searching and scrolling through data, scrolling through slides. AI and voice recognition will flip that dynamic. As the searching and scrolling through data is done for us -- as it follows our voice commands and conversations -- we get freed from our devices.

When our eyes are separated from a screen and are hands are freed from a keyboard, we are back in control of our lives. We can look up and around. Look at our friend, our business partner, the other people in the room. We can see them, talk with them and, above all, make a real connection with them. This is important in business, where having the latest gadget is a status symbol, but it's also a distraction. Everyone is so busy checking out your new Apple Watch that they forget about doing the new budget allocations. And it's even more important at the dinner table, where everyone is interacting with their phones instead of each other. Advances in AI, voice recognition and presentation technology will correct technology's worst flaws. They will free us from the devices and apps to which we've become enslaved, empower us to be more productive in our daily jobs, and above all allow us to connect with each other in a more meaningful way and form stronger bonds. That's progress.

The Humanity of Presentations: Cave Paintings to PowerPoint and Back Again

We've been presenting to each other before the word "present" ever made it into our vernacular. And we've forced ourselves to adjust and adapt to whatever technology was available at the time.

Cave paintings were likely the earliest form of presentation. Moses' Ten Commandments on two stone tablets were a form of presentation. Today, they might very well be two slides with five bullet points each. Then we evolved to paintings on wood and canvas, to still life photography and four-color printing, and then video.

In the latter half of the 20th century, businesses and universities relied on photographic slides shown on a Kodak Carousel. Slides were made of glass or film and were photographed and developed. After that, they were painstakingly placed in a specific order that could not be altered. Given the amount of work and skill required to create the slides, a presentation was a formal business event that usually took weeks to prepare. The lights were off so you could see the slides, and you'd hear the voice of the presenter, and the click of the carousel. Click-click, next slide please. Click-click. Next slide.

That gave way to the overhead projector with transparencies. Transparencies were faster and easier to create. You could write on them with a grease pen or even run them through a copy machine. The lead time required was much less than a slideshow, even though the quality was not as good. But again, the lights needed to be off so the audience could see the screen. The experience was a little mysterious and somewhat removed. The speaker was a voice in the dark. You couldn't see his face, and he couldn't see yours. And when the presentation ended, lights were turned back on. It was jarring as your eyes adjusted, like waking up from a cozy sleep because someone tore open the curtains.

Enter PowerPoint. Its first iteration was really a software form of the carousel – a slideshow. PowerPoint was, and still is, fast and easy, with lots of cool effects, animations, fonts, colors and charts. Where slideshows were once reserved for the most important presentations, PowerPoint could be used in all meetings because it was so easy and inexpensive that anyone could make a presentation. (Though, we admit, some are much better at it than others.) PowerPoint made slideshows mainstream. To this day, it remains such a powerful business tool that it has not only changed the way we present in meetings and classrooms, it has also changed the way we write, speak and communicate in general. Bullet points and outlines replaced long-form prose. Relying on slides, though misguided and certainly not recommended, became a crutch for spontaneous discussion and debate. While it made it easier to speak in front of a room, the rigid nature of a linear slide show replaced spontaneous discussion.

Yet spontaneous discussion, where we share our ideas with each other, is the best way to learn.

While PowerPoint was taking off in the early '90s, CD-ROM encyclopedias were also gaining popularity. CD-ROMs offered libraries of multimedia – pictures, video, text and other information – on a disc. They were a form of interactive, multimedia books. One of the first interactive books created for MGM was "James Bond – The Ultimate Interactive Dossier." It was an encyclopedic reference of all things James Bond. The explosive action shots, the different James Bond actors, the beautiful Bond girls, the evil villains, the stunning locations. Type in Pussy Galore and you'd be transported back to 1964 (before #MeToo) to read a synopsis and watch a video of Honor Blackman flying over Fort Knox in *Goldfinger*. It contained pictures, videos, story synopses and even a trivia game. You could play the CD on your computer and browse the library or do a keyword search to find your favorite villain. It was an interactive media library where all of the content was formatted to present – all the content was a slide. One interesting development from this was that James Bond aficionados would use the Dossier as a reference, as proof, as they were debating and discussing various James Bond storylines and characters. And although CD-ROMs soon became antiquated, this was an early example of the presentation following the conversation. These were great advances in presentation technology, but we were still tethered to a machine. We were a captive audience.

Now the Presentation Follows the Conversation

Better presentation strategy combined with technological advances is transforming presentations into enterprise assets – enterprise PowerPoint. Today, presentations are a mashup of all sorts of media and files – PowerPoints, but also images, videos, PDFs, Word, Excel, audio, etc. They are structured content, formatted as slides and ready to present. Presentations are now a branding element in the marketing mix, along with advertising, public relations, digital and collateral. Presentation content is designed, written, approved, executed and measured for the benefit of the entire organization, at the corporate level. Yet, the employees still maintain flexibility and control over their individual meetings and tasks. After all, who knows better what to present to a prospect than the salesperson who just had an in-depth conversation with that same prospect the week before the big meeting? Corporate marketing has control over the brand and message, and can track its use, while users in the field have flexibility. It's a win-win for both corporate marketing and the team in the field.

Advances in interactive technology have allowed presentations to be more conversational. Search and interactive features allow presenters to zoom into a particular slide, based on the feedback and cues that their audience members are giving them. No sooner does someone from the audience ask a question than the presenter is able to present content directly addressing the question. Presenters can build a presentation as they go, customizing directly to the mindset of the meeting attendees. Linear slideshows are becoming a thing of the past.

With presentation management, today's structured presentations follow the conversation.

But tomorrow, the conversation will dictate the presentation.

ACKNOWLEDGMENTS

AlexAnndra and James first and foremost want thank all of our clients -- those that have hired us and even fired us over the years. Their input and insights helped us learn and develop better presentation solutions, and ultimately provided the information that filled these pages.

We'd also like to thank our families and friends for their support over the years: April Darrow, Richard Darrow, Anne Phillips, Jeff Stewart, Fehmi Zeko, Bonnie Halper, Alison Malloy and Kristin Shevis who have listened to us harp, ruminate and contemplate as we labored through the process of running a business and writing a book.

Above all, a thank-you to Kevin Maney, who guided us and helped us put our ideas into words that someone might actually want to read.

AlexAnndra Ontra and James Ontra are co-founders of Shufflrr. The siblings grew up in Connecticut and then moved to Texas where AlexAnndra graduated from The University of Texas at Austin and James from the University of Houston. They have been business partners for over twenty years, developing presentation software and consulting with *Fortune* 1,000-level clients. They both live in New York City where Shufflrr is based.